Tony Hawthorne

TEAM MATES

Fairfield Books
17 George's Road, Bath BA1 6EY
Tel 01225-335813

First published 2016
Reprinted 2016

ISBN 978 0 9568511 7 8

Printed and bound in Great Britain by
CPI Antony Rowe, Bumpers Way, Chippenham, Wilts

TEAM MATES

edited by John Barclay
& Stephen Chalke

FAIRFIELD BOOKS

Contents

Special Thanks

We are most grateful to the Ernest Kleinwort Charitable
Trust and the Caldicott School Cricket Charity
whose most generous donations have covered
the full production costs of this book.

We are also most grateful to the book's 27 contributors,
all of whom have generously given their time without fee.

The result of their generosity is that *all* the money received
from the purchase of the book will go direct to the
Arundel Castle Cricket Foundation.

Acknowledgements

'Rahul Dravid' by Ed Smith appears
by kind permission of ESPNcricinfo.

'Jack Simmons' by David Lloyd appeared first
in 'G'day ya Pommie b.....!', published by
Weidenfeld and Nicolson in 1992.

Photographs

The photographs in this book appear
by kind permission of the following:

Arundel Castle Cricket Foundation: pages 8 and 9
Getty Images: pages 16, 21, 22, 30, 66, 70, 96,
118, 126, 129, 136, 158, 164, 176, 180 & 186
Gloucestershire CCC: page 46
Graeme Taylor: page 52
Mirrorpix: page 58
PA Images: page 76
Rex Photographs: page 80
Susanna Kendall: page 88
John Spencer: page 102
Glamorgan Cricket Archive: page 112
Sam Bowles: page 144
Sussex Cricket Museum: page 150
Andrew Wingfield Digby: page 170

This book
and the Arundel Castle Cricket Foundation

The Arundel Castle Cricket Foundation was formed thirty years ago in 1986. To mark this landmark and also to celebrate the work it has done, Stephen Chalke and I have persuaded distinguished writers from both the world of cricket and other walks of life to write about a favourite player with whom they have played cricket. And from that simple notion *Team Mates* has emerged from its chrysalis into a brightly-coloured book of charm and humour.

'Belonging' as part of a team is what many of us yearn for in life – not necessarily to be brilliant but to join in. That, I feel, is what we are all about at Arundel: giving young people, many with a variety of disadvantages, the chance to feel included. Many, many youngsters have now been visiting our lovely ground year after year – for all sorts of activities, games, some proper cricket and coaching, visits to the Castle, its gardens and the seaside. They love it and so do we. Accommodation nearby has for years now been a central part of the project and good food in the pavilion too – that is very popular and the source of much and important social interaction and chat. Young people getting to know each other is so important.

In thirty years we have encouraged and given our special Arundel enthusiasm to thousands – no, hundreds of thousands – of young people, whose lives have been enriched and enhanced by their experiences. Thank you all for your support and for buying a book which will help to ensure that we can extend the best possible opportunities to the young in the future.

Thank you so much.

John Barclay
Director of Cricket and Coaching
Arundel Castle Cricket Foundation

The Arundel Castle Cricket Foundation

The purpose of the Foundation is to enhance the development and education of young people, with a special emphasis upon the disadvantaged, the disabled and those deprived of opportunity. It concentrates on the inner cities, particularly London's boroughs where the need has been greatest, using cricket to achieve its aims. The ground at Arundel is at the heart of the project, and there are also tours of the Castle and gardens, trips to the seaside and – for some groups – overnight stays.

Arundel Castle Cricket Foundation

Donations can be made by post to
Arundel Castle Cricket Foundation
Arundel Park
West Sussex
BN18 9LH

or by paying into the
Arundel Castle Cricket Foundation bank account:

NatWest – Littlehampton branch
Sort code: 60-01-18
Account number: 46079068

Introduction
by Stephen Chalke

> Cricket is a game of the most terrifying stresses with more luck
> about it than any other game. They call it a team game but in
> fact it is the loneliest game of all.   *John Arlott*

Other games have moments when the individual is on their own, carrying
the hopes of the team: the footballer stepping forward in the penalty shoot-
out, the Ryder Cup golfer standing over the match-winning putt, the rugby
player poised to kick the crucial conversion. But no other team game is
constructed so relentlessly out of individual performances. At every moment
of action the great majority of the 22 participants are merely spectators.

Take poor Fred Tate in his only Test for England – against Australia
at Old Trafford in 1902, a match that would settle the destination of that
summer's Ashes series. The captain, Archie MacLaren, made clear that he
had not wanted him in the side. At a crucial moment in the Australian
second innings Tate was sent out of the slips to field on the boundary,
where he was never at ease, and immediately he found himself under a
swirling catch that he dropped. Then on the last afternoon, under a dark
sky, he walked out to bat, last man in with eight runs required for victory.
And, as if the tension of that moment were not enough, it started to rain,
and the umpires took them off. For forty minutes he sat in the dressing
room, waiting to play his part in victory or defeat. Whatever they may have
said to him – "Play straight ... Leave it to Wilfred" – he was on his own.

There are few better experiences in sport than that moment when as
an individual you win a game for your team and come off to the warm
applause of your team-mates. Everybody loves you. And there are few worse
moments than when you mess it up, when you drop the vital catch or play
the wrong shot, and that mistake results in the narrowest of defeats. Then
the team-mates turn away and mutter. I know, I have been there, been to
both places. Triumph or disaster, the line is so thin – and it is so much
harder that you are doing it not just for yourself but for the team.

Fred Tate dabbed his first ball for four, blocked the next two, then
found himself unable to keep out the quicker fourth ball. His leg stump
somersaulted out of the ground, and England had lost – by three runs.

In the railway station buffet, waiting for his train home, the crowds
pointed at him and muttered. He was the man who had lost the Ashes; that
was for ever to be his cricketing fate. More than a century has passed, and
still the game is known as Fred Tate's Match.

So what are the elements of team work that can help us as individual cricketers to cope with such moments? Or are there none?

The germ of this book was sown in the aftermath of the Great Debate about Kevin Pietersen. He was arguably England's best player, yet it was decided that the team would do better without his talent. How could that be in a game where so much of success depends on individual contributions? What was the nature of his disruption that it took more away from the team than were added by the runs he scored?

It struck me that such questions only get asked when there are problems. Why not come at this from the other end? Why not ask some cricketers to write about team-mates with whom they enjoyed playing, and to reflect on what those team-mates gave to their fellow cricketers that was positive? And, better still, why not do the whole thing for charity, to support a cause that is all about team work, about giving the most vulnerable and disadvantaged a sense of belonging?

John Barclay and I set to work, compiling a list of people to ask. Some were chosen because we knew them to be good writers, some because they would offer something distinctive, some were friends. Some had played cricket at the highest level of the men's or women's game; others had got no further than the village green. Thus five England captains nestle alongside captains of the Stage Cricket Club and the Harry Baldwin Occasionals.

We were delighted by the positive response. More than three-quarters of those asked – despite demanding schedules – agreed to write. We were also delighted not only by the quality of their contributions but by the variety. Some wrote about the greats of cricket with whom they had had the pleasure to play; others celebrated lesser lights. Some wrote exclusively about a single character; others broadened out to explore themes. One shone a rare light on the world of second-eleven county cricket, where team work is mingled with the rivalry of ambition. Another chose to observe a team-mate relationship of which he was not a part. And one, interpreting the task with the greatest freedom of all, told the tale of *Cricket*, a rare musical entertainment.

At one level this book is simply a collection of 27 essays, each one to be enjoyed for itself. You are witness to the extraordinary routine of Alan Knott getting himself ready for a day's play; then you are running between the wickets with Zaheer Abbas. You are under the spell of that great gentleman of cricket, Rahul Dravid; then you are in the Swan at Swinbrook with the local skip driver.

Yet patterns do emerge.

One is the number of writers who have chosen for their subjects men and women from different backgrounds – and cultures – from their own. Six of those who played county cricket have selected overseas players – so we discover the joys of a young Paul Parker, a Cambridge University undergraduate, breaking into the Sussex team at the same time as an even younger Javed Miandad from the back streets of Karachi; David Gower, a fresh-faced public schoolboy, alongside Brian Davison, a hard-living veteran of the no-holds-barred Rhodesian civil war; Chesterfield-born Geoff Miller having his cricketing horizons widened beyond the time-worn routine of the 1970s county game by the South African Eddie Barlow. Then, among those who have chosen an English subject, there is Rachael Heyhoe Flint, a Tory peer, celebrating her team-mate Enid Bakewell, an unwavering Labour Party member who grew up among the collieries of Nottinghamshire.

A cricket season lasts a long time, especially when you play professionally and you are cooped up every day with the same people. It can help if your team contains characters who are out of the ordinary, whose presence prevents the routine becoming dull. Some are in this book: Alan Knott, Jack Simmons, the young Rodney Marsh. It can also help if you have team-mates who have as positive a spirit on a damp day at Derby as on a sun-drenched one at Lord's. Here we have John Lever, bowling day in, day out and never giving second best, and we have Eddie Hemmings, on the verge of going out of the professional game, yet finding his way back from the graveyard of second-eleven cricket through his undimmed enthusiasm.

T20 cricket may be too fast-moving for such matters to come into play, but the county championship is a long, winding road; it needs commitment on the dull days in April as much as in the key contests of high summer. When Ray Illingworth was signed up to captain Leicestershire, he was quick to pension off the old lags who were at their happiest playing cards in the pavilion – and, with young blood and some well-chosen recruits, he won the county its first championship.

Perhaps that match at Old Trafford would have worked out better for poor Fred Tate if he had had a greater sense that he was wanted by his captain and that he belonged among the England cricketers. So the team-mate who makes the newcomer welcome can play a vital role. Few can have made a more humiliating start to their county careers than the young John Barclay, as he tells so vividly in his piece, but the kindness of John Spencer saw him through to better days.

As a batsman you are not entirely on your own – you have a partner – and there is the potential for team-work in that. Bryan Stott writes poignantly about his Yorkshire opening partner Ken Taylor, how their mutual trust strengthened their cricket and how it has remained with them in a lifelong friendship.

Roy Smith played 96 times for Somerset as a batsman, but his only century came in a game when initially he struggled with the swing and seam of the veteran Reg Perks. His partner Harold Gimblett summoned him at the end of one over: "Come here, son. Are you having a bit of a problem down there? … I'll tell you what. I'll look after Perksy for a few overs. You come down this end." Gimblett duly hit three or four fours, then said, "There you are, son. He might be a bit easier for you now."

It was a different approach from that of Len Hutton who, only half in jest, responded to praise of a gutsy innings by Lancashire's Jack Ikin against the fast bowling of South Africa's Cuan McCarthy by saying, "He could have played him better." "How's that, Len?" they asked, to which he replied, "He could have stayed down the other end."

Or the story, strongly denied by Geoffrey Boycott, that out in Australia he once told his partner Basil D'Oliveira, who had just worked out how to play Johnny Gleeson, the mystery spinner, "Yes, I figured that out an hour ago – but don't tell the others." In all probability the story is apochryphal, a misunderstanding of an ill-phrased comment, but it is doubtful if it would ever have gained currency if whatever was said had come from John Edrich or D'Oliveira himself. When you play cricket with somebody, you soon know where they are on the spectrum of playing for themselves or playing for the team. Often, of course, the two are not in conflict – but not always.

There is nobody alive with a better overview of post-war English cricket than Micky Stewart. His early years in the first-class game were as part of the triumphant Surrey side who won seven successive championships in the 1950s so he knew from the start what it was like to play in a team that went into every game expecting to win. Yet he is clear that, outside Yorkshire and Surrey, there was not at that time the same importance attached to the result. There was more emphasis on individual performances.

The game has moved on since then, and among the changes has been a much greater attention to fitness and preparation. Each fielder is trained to give their all throughout the day, diving to save every run on the boundary as if the game depended on it. A good fielding side can create pressure on batsmen, and even one weak link can undermine that. So here is fresh opportunity for coaches and trainers to work with the team as a group.

But, as Mark Wagh asks in his piece, is the modern emphasis on team bonding overdone, the product of coaches desperate to make a difference?

In the end, is not the important thing to score runs and take wickets? Would you ever pick a good bloke, a reliable team man, ahead of somebody who would score you an extra five or ten runs each innings?

Perhaps the answer varies according to the cricket you play. At the level I played, the first and most important definition of a good team man is that he is reliable; he makes himself available to play when you need him and he doesn't drop out at the last minute.

What is a good team-mate? There is no one answer, but – in asking the writers to reflect on people whose presence added to the spirit of the team – there are pointers. Cricket is a long game, and the company you keep while you play is undoubtedly part of the experience.

Winning teams do tend to be happier than losing ones. There is general agreement on that. But are happy teams more likely to win than unhappy ones? This book cannot answer that question, but it does make one thing clear, over and over again. Cricket, at its best, is a game that can bring people together and create friendship. Unlike in, say, golf, the efforts of cricketers are always part of a collective endeavour, and that gives the playing of the game a special quality. You strive for your own moments of success but, if you only play for yourself, if you gain no great joy from the success of your team-mates, it is a long day and a long season. It *is* a team game.

I will never forget the words of the late Tom Cartwright about the day when he played at the ancient ground on Broadhalfpenny Down in a match to celebrate the 70th birthday of his former Warwickshire and England team-mate Bob Barber. The field was filled with men who forty years earlier had been stars of the game, and they had come from far and wide – Australians, West Indians, Pakistanis – to renew their friendships.

"It was a magical day," Tom said. "A living evidence of what is really good about playing cricket. When you looked at the different backgrounds of all the people there and the way they'd come together in cricket and played on equal terms, it really brought home what cricket can be in people's lives."

It may be true, as John Arlott wrote, that cricket has moments of 'terrifying stress' and that it is at times 'the loneliest game of all'. In its long hours of anticipation and action, it tests and reveals character like no other game.

So much of cricket focuses on individual performances, and they are crucial. Yet, when you play, you are always aware of the team-mates around you, and those team-mates can shape your experience of the game for better or worse.

Here in these pages are a few examples of the 'better'.

15

Angus Fraser

Angus Fraser

by Mike Atherton

Mike Atherton played cricket for Cambridge University (1987-89), Lancashire (1987-2001) and England (115 Tests, 1989-2001, 54 as captain). He is now the cricket correspondent of *The Times* and is a member of the Sky television broadcasting team.

Angus Fraser played cricket for Middlesex (1984-2002) and England (46 Tests, 1989-98). He is now Managing Director of Cricket at Middlesex and an England selector.

'Team-mate'. It's a curious word in cricket, isn't it? After all, it is a cliché that one of the glories of the game is its property of being, essentially, an individual pursuit carried out within the framework of a team. And mates? Those you play with are work colleagues first and foremost. They can become great mates, but they are work colleagues above all, from whom and for whom respect rather than absolute friendship is a starting point.

For all the guff spouted by coaches, managers, consultants and leadership gurus, everyone who has played the game knows that great players win matches. It was Richie Benaud who said that if you have one truly great player in a team you will win matches; two truly great players will win you more matches than you lose. Glenn McGrath and Shane Warne, anyone? Give me two great bowlers over any intangible benefits of the baggy green culture.

And yet, and yet. Good, great teams become so because they add up to more than the sum of their parts. These things are hard to quantify. While I will always be an advocate of the Steve Archibald school of team spirit ('an illusion glimpsed in the aftermath of victory') most professional cricketers will have experienced both good and bad 'teams' – and not in the winning or losing sense. The modern buzzword is 'culture': some dressing rooms you look forward to walking into, some you don't.

For years, I felt that the Lancashire team that I played in throughout the 1980s and 1990s benefited from the shared upbringing and togetherness of so many of the players. When I joined the staff in 1987 I did so with seven players I had played with in junior teams, and there were half-a-dozen more whom I had come across from time to time. We were friends; we shared memories; we shared similar backgrounds; we had known each other at school; our parents knew each other. We identified with the county and what it meant to be a Lancashire player. Then again, we might have won so many one-day trophies because we had such good players. Who can truly know where the balance lies?

*

The first Fraser I got to know was not Angus but Alastair, his younger brother. At that stage I didn't really know about Gus, because Alastair was the star of the family, the bowler destined for great things. He was tall, lithe, whippy and quick. Think, perhaps, of Neil Foster from Essex and get the idea of the bowler Alastair might have become, had things gone to plan.

We went on tour together to Sri Lanka with Young England in the winter of 1987, and within two years I would be playing in an Ashes Test for England – with Alastair's brother, Gus. Perhaps the physical differences between them – Gus was heavier boned, less obviously athletic – had allowed Gus to skip under the radar compared with his brother. But the hard graft and grind of county cricket suited Gus well, as did the successful Middlesex team that he found himself in.

Whenever we (Lancashire, that is) played Middlesex I always felt that the two dressing rooms were not dissimilar. That is to say, that they were player led, rather than coach led, and dominated by some very strong characters. Lancashire had Paul Allott and Graeme Fowler, Middlesex had Mike Gatting, Desmond Haynes, Wayne Daniel. It was not unusual at Lancashire to find ourselves arguing furiously before, during or after matches. Sometimes, the arguments went too far and ended physically. It was a robust dressing room and players were encouraged to air their views, even if, in keeping with the time, it was a touch hierarchical.

So we came from similar county dressing rooms. But what brought us a little closer after the first tour we went on together with England (Australia '90/91) was injury. Gus had gone in the hip and many thought that was because of the excessive overs he was bowling, given that he had very quickly become the leader and most dependable member of the attack. Me? I'd gone in the back, excruciating pains from my sacroiliac joint downwards, firstly diagnosed as a stress fracture (which was there but not causing the problem) but later as an auto-immune condition. I remember us meeting up after the tour ended in a hospital in Nottingham, he in some kind of cast and limping with the aid of a stick, me unable to bend down, with a screw positioned in my lower back to no effect. Quite a couple.

It was a worrying time. More so for him, I reckon, because try as they might, the medics could not get to the bottom of his hip injury. Was it a stress fracture? Was it lack of blood flow? Was it wear and tear? Who knew? At least a simple blood test sorted out my diagnosis after which various anti-inflammatories and steroids allowed me to kick-start my career again. For a while, our paths diverged. I got back into the England team and became captain; Gus, finally fit again, trod the county championship boards, seemingly a shadow of his former self.

Perhaps the best bit of news I got as captain came during my second selection meeting. We had lost the first match under my captaincy – making a run of about ten defeats in a row at that stage – and we were desperately trying to come up with a formula to stop the bleeding. Ted Dexter was the chairman of selectors and he arrived on his motorbike, as was his way, stripped off his leathers and sat down to read the averages. By and by, he looked up and announced that he'd just seen the best bowler in county cricket this year. His name? Angus Fraser. Ted reckoned he was not quite back to his very best, but damn near so. That was good enough for me. It was the easiest and happiest selection I was involved in.

We won the next Test match at the Oval – Gus bowled beautifully and took wickets – and took a team to the Caribbean of which Gus was an integral part. He remained so, on and off – sometimes more on than off – for the next few years of my captaincy. I can't say that I valued a team-mate more.

*

His personal example was outstanding. I cannot remember a time that he did not give his absolute all on the field. Of course, playing for your country, that should be a natural state of affairs, but all players go through phases – and I'm not talking about 'form' here – where off-the-field problems impact upon their state of mind and ability to focus and concentrate. It always seemed to me that Gus gave his all to every ball that he bowled.

I can well remember, during the Sydney Test of '95, he bowled his heart out, having, one assumed, a point to prove to the selectors who had left him out of the original touring party. After a trying spell in humid weather, he found himself fielding at short third man; a late cut skimmed past him and as he went to chase he began to get cramp. It didn't stop him, though, and he limped to the ball and threw it back in, refusing to yield. No-one could not have been inspired by his example that day.

In and around the dressing room, he was a valuable source of honest reaction. One of the earliest changes I noticed as captain was that other players became more guarded when they spoke in my company, less willing to be as direct or critical as they had previously been for fear of upsetting someone who might have some influence to bear on selection. Of course, it was not always easy to see that change at the time, but looking back I can see it clearly now.

Gus, though, remained loyal. Not loyal to me, but loyal to his instincts, his need for honesty and directness. He was quite happy to tell me when I behaved foolishly. In that Sydney Test, for example, he was quite clear that he thought I had messed up in declaring on Graeme Hick. He was not afraid to criticise selections I made or field placings, or the content of team-talks. Leaders must never fight shy of surrounding themselves with people who will hold them to account and tell them things they may not wish to hear. It is so valuable.

In a different era – now, for example, when bowlers are protected from the grind of county cricket – Gus would have taken more than the 177 Test wickets he ended up with. A fair reflection of his ability and his value to the England team of the time would be another 80 or so. A 250-wicket man would be about right. But there were no central contracts, there were no directives telling bowlers to rest up before Test matches, only county captains desperate to get bonus points or win cup matches. Still, what most of us hope for at the end of a career is respect from the players we played with and played against, and Gus is certainly held in the highest esteem.

*

Our paths have converged and diverged since then. He went into the press box initially and did the job diligently but is much happier, I think, in his current role as Middlesex director of cricket. His heart was always happiest in and around the dressing room. We bump into each other now and then: my lad plays junior cricket with Middlesex and so I see him around the scene, and, of course, I see him in his role as selector. I wince if I have to write something critical about the England selection panel but, deep down, I know he would expect nothing less than an honest assessment, providing the comment is fair, and I know that if the roles were reversed he wouldn't hold back either.

Angus Fraser (left) and Mike Atherton

Alan Knott

Alan Knott

by Chris Cowdrey

Chris Cowdrey played cricket for Kent (1976-91), Glamorgan (1992) and England (1984-88, 6 Tests, one as captain). He is now an accomplished master of ceremonies and after-dinner speaker.

Alan Knott played cricket for Kent (1964-85) and England (1967-81, 95 Tests). In 2013 *Wisden Cricketers' Almanack* named him as the wicket-keeper in its all-time Test World XI. He now lives in Cyprus.

The sportsmen I have enjoyed most tend to have similar qualities. Attacking, funny, eccentric, with a freakish talent – which, when choosing my favourite team-mate, led me to think of David Gower. If I had played for Chelsea in the early '70s, it would have been Peter Osgood or Alan Hudson. But strangely, whilst I adore the reckless maverick, I haven't chosen one.

Let me talk you through a day in the life of the greatest wicket-keeper/batsman and nicest guy of all time, Alan Knott. To understand him you have to bear in mind that he was a genius. Philosopher David Hume believed that 'a person with the characteristics of a genius is looked at as a person disconnected from society, as well as a person who works remotely, at a distance.' Decide for yourself.

It is a warm June morning in Herne Bay, with a slight breeze off the sea and the smell of oysters drifting in from Whitstable. Knotty sets off on the 20-minute journey to the St Lawrence Ground, Canterbury, in his old Volvo estate. Now there's a story in itself.

Knotty has always driven this Volvo, ever since I have known him. He likes it because the seats are harder than most and good for his posture – although he always drives with a couple of big cushions behind his back. The only alteration over a decade has been to the accelerator. He has attached a block of wood to it, rather like the business end of a croquet mallet. This limits the movement required by his right leg when accelerating and protects his Achilles tendon.

As a leading English sportsman he has been offered brand new Jaguars, Mercedes, BMWs – the lot. But he has stuck with his old Volvo. So, yes, he is eccentric.

Before getting in the car he always listens to the television weather, swearing that Francis on Breakfast Time is the greatest forecaster of them all. So on this glorious sunny morning he arrives at the ground in an old fisherman's hat and coat, with his collar up to protect his neck from the imaginary wind. Francis has predicted cooler weather and possible rain later. It is a scorcher.

The team has a pre-match training session, but Knotty always does a much longer warm-up on his own. He religiously loosens up every part of his body before taking a few gentle underarm throws into each glove. He will never take part in a fielding practice where young upstarts like me hurl the ball in for fun. Keepers have always done this, but he never does because his delicate hands are his livelihood.

Rarely will he spend much time batting in the nets, but when he does it is always an unusual experience. I bowled the first ball to him one day, and he slogged it miles over mid-wicket. "Why the hell did you do that?" I said. "Sorry," he replied. "I forgot to tell you; I am practising for the Sunday League tomorrow."

We lose the toss and we are fielding. Now for the grand performance of getting him ready in the 30 minutes before play. He gives us a running commentary on the weather conditions, still not believing the rain hasn't arrived, and the problem he is going to have to be ready. "Is that the time already?" he repeats every ten minutes. He sips his tea, which has been sitting there since he went out to practise. Hot tea could give him stomach cramps, so he fills the cup three-quarters full with milk before adding a spoonful of Romanian honey. Only Romanian – something to do with "special acacia or lime honey, due to the favourable natural conditions". I watch him in awe, as I dunk my digestive biscuits into a boiling-hot builder's tea. There is something special about having a 'legend' changing next to you, even if he does take up half the room.

Progress, with still 20 minutes to go – in white pants and vest, it is time for the baggy long-sleeved shirt. Always long sleeves to protect his elbows from grass burns, but with a difference. On the wall he has many different length strips of plaster. The small ones do up his cuffs where he has cut off the buttons; the newly made cuff-links prevent the shirt being too tight on his wrists.

Another sip of the same cup of tea, with some retort like "Ouch, the tea's a bit warm!" On with the white trousers which don't really have any special trademarks except for the handkerchief which always rests half out of his right-hand pocket. This simplifies the process of blowing his nose – no struggling to get the handkerchief out of the pocket with sweaty inner gloves.

The wicket-keeping pads follow a similar procedure to the shirt. He has cut off the middle buckles which could directly irritate his calf muscles all day. He's replaced them with the plaster bandage which is wrapped right around the front of the pad. At this stage you have to wonder whether you are really looking at one of the greatest in the history of the game.

The five-minute bell goes. "No, is that the bell? I can't believe it!" Now, just in time for the pièce de résistance. The famous hat and gloves come out of the case. Famous for different reasons. The sun hat which has been repaired so many times over the years, deliberately weighed down by thick tape so as to stay on his head if and when Francis's windy conditions arrive. The red Slazenger gloves are the epitome of Knotty and, extraordinarily, are the same pair of gloves he has used around the world for many years.

On they go, all taped up, as we exit the dressing room with his cries of "I'm nearly ready, don't go without me" ringing out behind us. We never wait for him because he won't take practice throws on the field anyway so we don't need him.

Once on the field we do need him – eccentric but what a genius. Sometimes he is the only one not to appeal for an LBW: "I think it was just sliding down the leg-side." Then on another occasion he will be the only one on the field to think it was out. Knotty does produce remarkable performances every day, and in all the years I can honestly say I cannot remember him dropping a catch standing back.

Knotty didn't like standing up to the seamers. He felt the wasted opportunity, dropping the thick edge, outweighed any pressure standing up might have put on the batsman. However, standing up to Derek 'Deadly' Underwood was what proved him to be the greatest wicket-keeper of all time. I was in the box seat, travelling first-class at silly point for seven years, witnessing one of the greatest cricketing partnerships at work. Knott and Underwood – wow!

On uncovered pitches, when a wet surface under a burning sun made Underwood unplayable, you would have thought if the batsmen couldn't cope, then the poor old keeper would have struggled. I cannot picture him missing a ball, sometimes taking it high above his head. More often than not after a freak take he would turn to his silly point fielder with a big grin: "I was pleased with that one."

Knotty, unsurprisingly, read Deadly better than anyone and was a great judge of what pace he should bowl on a certain pitch. He wasn't like the vocal modern keeper. He never ever abused an opposition player. In fact, you never heard him at all, but he was always in the game.

So we come off at lunchtime after a flawless keeping display. "I can't believe it hasn't rained." The routine never changes. A cheese roll, a pot of tea with Bucharest honey and on hot days maybe a very flat coke (which shouldn't upset his tummy). It has been a bad morning with not much happening for the bowlers, yet as always he comes out with the same sort of strangely inspirational comment: 'Wouldn't it be nice to have one of those sessions where it swings and we get nine wickets?'

He will quietly encourage players to think they are better than they really are. He often said to me, "You should be bowling, you would bowl really well on this pitch." I would feel good about it for an hour or so. Then I would start to wonder what pitch I might ever bowl particularly well on.

There is a similar pattern for the afternoon session during which the 12th man gets increasingly busy bringing on Knotty's drinks. I used to feel so sorry for him on hot days with all the garb on but he never moaned about it. After the 20-minute tea break on every single day of his career, he would shriek: "This is the best session, lads, 'cos it's the last one!"

Finally we are back in the dressing room at close of play and, unlike some players who have evening plans, he will sit there recuperating from six hours behind the stumps. The 12th man or dressing-room attendant brings in everyone's drink to order. They range from pints of lager, milk, orange & lemonade – Deadly and I will have a pint of bitter, unless he has bowled 35 overs, then it's a bitter top.

And then there is HIM! Knotty will have a pint of sherry & lemonade. I often think he only does it to be funny because he doesn't drink. The sherry is at the bottom, and he sips about half of the rest off the top. "I feel a bit queasy," he says.

Most of the players have showered and changed before Knotty has eventually managed to strip off. This isn't just today, this is every day when we have been in the field. Into the shower – never a soak in the bath, as he doesn't see the point of 'washing in your own dirt'. By the time he has dressed back into hat and coat, not even the most hardened supporter will have waited for his autograph.

So back to Herne Bay in the Volvo.

I travelled with him once to Yorkshire in that dreadful motor. It wasn't long after the M25 and the Dartford Tunnel had trimmed hours off our travels north from Canterbury. However, I nodded off for a while and woke to find that we were in a traffic jam in Peckham, South London, nearing rush hour. I enquired why we hadn't joined the M25 Dartford Tunnel and Knotty simply said, "I never go that way because I always stop at the Cumberland Hotel at the top of Park Lane to break up the journey."

Oh my God, a four-hour drive would now be in excess of six hours and eating into valuable pint-of-Tetley's drinking time. Knotty's eating habit was always the same – two poached eggs, some bread and butter and, you've guessed it, a pot of tea. He always stopped at The Cumberland, which is why I stopped travelling with him.

Two interesting things happened in Yorkshire. We were involved in a run chase in the cup at Headingley, and Knotty and I were going well until Arnie Sidebottom returned. He set a leg-side field to Knotty, firing it in to his pads. At the end of the over Knotty said, "What can I do?" My advice was for him to open up his stance and smash the ball over mid-wicket.

"I am better going the other way," he said, and promptly jumped outside leg stump and ran the ball off the face of the bat behind leg stump past the right hand of keeper David Bairstow for four. An extraordinary shot, way before Dilshan or AB de Villiers were even born.

Then in Scarborough, towards the end of his last season, we were cruising a Sunday League match, when he lost confidence in his batting on a low pitch. We only needed a few to win, but he didn't back himself to slog across the line and he couldn't score. He finished up being run out on the last ball, and we lost by 0.025 of a run! The dressing room was in silence. What do you say to the world's greatest who never lets you down, when he has just let you down? I think he was in tears.

Many Kentish folk shed a tear when that season of 1985 came to an end. Sadly after Scarborough Alan Knott only played one more championship match, against Worcestershire at New Road, and one more Sunday League match, against Derbyshire at Folkestone, and both times he was run out – for 1 and 0. Running between the wickets and in particular calling for a run was never his strong suit.

Just occasionally Knotty's theories didn't make sense, but mostly they worked for him. His belief that you should sweep a left-arm spinner every ball seemed fun, and he was very good at it, so it took hold of me. I couldn't stop sweeping and forgot to hit the ball straight ever again.

I have fond personal memories of Knotty identifying a slow pitch and immediately saying, "Cow, this is made for you, it's a big man's wicket." He was so right. Class players like Bob Woolmer sometimes struggled to get the ball off the square on dead pitches, but sloggers like me …

Yet, on bouncy pitches, who can forget Knotty's entertaining yet eccentric batting against the likes of Lillee and Thomson, carving the ball over the slip cordon to five Test centuries?

Knotty's first ever Kent coach, Colin Page, would have found it hard to believe that he would go on to play 95 Test matches. During his debut as a keeper in the Kent second XI 'Pagey' the captain was bowling his off spin and warned young Knott (who had signed as an off-spin bowler himself) that, when he dropped his left arm to his side on the way back to his mark, it would be the signal for the quicker ball. A few balls into the next over the signal came and Knotty ran back ten yards to receive the quicker ball before Pagey had even turned. The expletives that followed are for another day!

Alan Knott is ingrained in the record books as cricket's most special keeper/batsman on the strength of his remarkable keeping. In this short account of the great man I may have painted a picture of an individual obsessed with his own performance, a hypochondriac, a freak, an introvert but his cheery influence in the dressing room was emphatic.

I would like to have chosen a real unsung hero, but as a team man Knotty was an unsung hero. He dedicated his efforts to winning for the team.

Above all he is the most modest man I know; he never says a bad word about anyone, he has a delightful wife Jan and son James. In 1984 I was selected to tour India with England, and at the hotel awaiting my arrival in Bombay there was a telegram which read: 'Good luck Chris, show them how good you are. Love Alan & Jan.'

I am proud to be able to say he is my friend and once upon a time a very special team-mate.

Chris Tavaré

Chris Tavaré

by Vic Marks

Vic Marks played cricket for Oxford University (1975-78), Somerset (1975-89) and England (6 Tests, 1982-84). He now writes on cricket for the *Guardian* and *Observer* newspapers and is a member of the *Test Match Special* team.

Chris Tavaré played cricket for Oxford University (1975-77), Kent (1974-88), Somerset (1989-92) and England (31 Tests, 1980-89). He now teaches Biology at Sevenoaks School.

A favourite team-mate? There are a few candidates, some of them very familiar, some misunderstood, some sadly no longer with us. All of them have made me realise, while tiptoeing as slowly as possible towards my dotage, how lucky I have been to be able to count them as team-mates. Most of them played for Somerset somewhere along the way.

I'm most often asked about Ian Botham and Viv Richards, with whom I began my time as a professional cricketer for Somerset. The short answer is that on their good days they were without parallel.

We knew Richards was phenomenal right from the start. I remember the first middle practice at Taunton in April 1974. A cheerful, earnest pace bowler by the name of Bob Clapp, who would become an even better teacher, charged in; Richards rocked forward and then back and square cut with awesome certainty. As the ball smashed into the boundary boards Peter Roebuck and I looked at one another in tacit agreement. We were not going to get into the team ahead of this man.

Viv cared about any team he played for. He liked winning matches more than scoring runs. The more important the match, the more likely that he would decide it. I remember how he was aghast when Geoffrey Boycott once suggested to him that he could get "a nice little not out" in the fourth innings of a county fixture against Yorkshire. Richards could never play the game that way.

Viv cared for his partners when at the crease – with the odd proviso. There was always the temptation to abnegate responsibility when batting with Richards, to leave him to do all the run-scoring. He did not like that – and he was right. If you were prepared to join him in the challenge rather than play the parasite, Viv would help you all he could.

So would Botham, even if in the early days he did not seem such an obvious source of advice. When he was setting out as a pro he demanded attention because we recognised that anything might happen. We did not, however, realise that we were alongside England's greatest all-rounder and a future knight of the realm.

Roebuck and I were operating the scoreboard at Taunton when Ian produced an early epic against Hampshire in a B&H quarter-final in June 1974. Minus the odd tooth and with a blood-stained shirt after being hit by a bouncer from Andy Roberts, Botham, batting at nine, cracked 45 not out, thereby managing to conjure an unlikely victory for his team. This was probably the first time he had done this on the public stage, but it would not be the last. Such was the excitement inside the scoreboard that two imminent Oxbridge undergraduates completely lost control of the mathematics of the match and were roundly – and justly – abused by 6,500 spectators.

Roebuck, with whom I got hilariously lost – so it now seems – on various haphazard car journeys around the country, often while he was berating a misguided panellist on *Any Questions*, is no longer with us; nor from that Somerset side is Peter Denning, who died from cancer in 2007. Both in contrasting ways were cherished team-mates. Of the two Roebuck was a little more analytical in his assessment of opponents since Denning's standard contribution to rare team meetings was "Let's stuff the bastards." Ask him to articulate his batting philosophy and he would reply, "If it's there, it's got to go." He batted with what Botham called a 'Swan Vesta', so light was his bat, and he revelled in playing the 'Chewton Chop'. His cut shot would often beat a brace of third men.

Denning was not as much of a country bumpkin as he liked to make out. In fact he was a qualified teacher, probably the solitary MCC member in the side, at least until Nigel Popplewell arrived, and he had a shrewd cricketing brain underneath his thatch of blond hair. He was great to bat with since he was selfless – he would not leave you stranded at Croft's/Clarke's/Roberts' end if he could help it – and he was a superb judge of a run. And if ever you felt like a nightcap and a consoling chat after the latest failure, he would be guaranteed to be at the bar.

Away from Somerset there is a special place in the scrapbook of my mind for Graeme Fowler, not just because his old man somehow managed to fix my car when Graeme and I were engaged at Headingley making our Test debuts together in 1982. Foxy's mind – and his body for that matter – was seldom static even at night; he could talk and he could sleep walk. When he talked he was never dull – such is the unpredictable fertility of his brain; when he walked in his sleep he was mildly terrifying.

Graeme became great mates with the man that I have decided will occupy most of my space here. Chris Tavaré was a team-mate in my first first-class match – for Oxford University in April 1975 – and in my last one – for Somerset in September 1989. We also played a little together for England.

We first met when we were selected for ESCA (English Schools Cricket Association) in 1973. Chris stood tall and drove handsomely on either side of the wicket with remarkable power. To me he seemed the best player in the side. We ended up in the same Oxford college, St John's, in September 1974, and thereafter we would meet most evenings for a pint in the same Oxford pub, *The Eagle and Child*. Our conversations may not have been as wide-ranging as those of CS Lewis and JRR Tolkien – there was a plaque there to remind us that this was one of their favourite haunts. Lewis and Tolkien probably did not dally too long on the merits of taking a middle and leg guard as opposed to centre.

Chris was no ascetic. He liked to share the odd drink. Once he drank me under the table in a Wellington hotel after a long Test match against New Zealand. I'm sure he must have cheated after I had decided that what his poor batting form needed was a post-Test blow-out. The only difference between us on those occasions back in Oxford was that, when we raised our glasses, Chris was usually celebrating the completion of his latest piece of work, while I was still seeking inspiration for mine.

In 1976 Chris played some brilliant innings for the University, full of flowing drives that impressed the most demanding of judges. He would stand at second slip – because that is where we reckoned most edges would go – and he would gently embrace the ball with the softest hands imaginable. And he would offer sage advice, which was nearly always followed, to a harassed university captain.

Before long we were in the same England dressing room. Please note that Tavaré was first picked for England as a one-day cricketer, and in his first match he made a gutsy 82 not out in a low-scoring game against the West Indies at Headingley in 1980. However, soon his reputation as a blocker was immutable.

He did change his technique, which had seemed so simple in his early university days. This was most notable in the way he gripped the bat. He opted for the 'Kent grip' as advocated by Bob Woolmer and Alan Knott. The left hand was an awfully long way around the handle; this may have helped to play the steeply bouncing deliveries of the West Indian fast bowlers, which were the source of the greatest concern for batsmen in that era. But it also restricted the range of strokes available. It was an unusual way to hold the bat and it may explain why Chris once told me that Paul Azinger was his favourite golfer – "He's got a funny grip too."

Bob Willis as England captain loved having Tavaré in his side because he hated profligate batsmen and he wanted time to rest those wonky knees. But I have often wondered whether Chris adopted the best approach as an England player. He would say, "I wish I could bat like Lubo [*David Gower*] or Gatt [*Mike Gatting*], but I can't." My view has always been that he was better than he thought. On a couple of occasions in his Test career he slipped anchor as a batsman: against Australia at Melbourne in 1982 – the game when his hands were not quite so soft at the end, but fortunately

Geoff Miller was on hand to help out – and when delivering a match-winning innings against Sri Lanka in their inaugural Test in Colombo.

He would occasionally block at county level as well. When Chris played at Taunton for Kent Ian Botham, who thought the world of his sleeping partner of Old Trafford 1981, would taunt him from slip when I was bowling. "Come on, Rowdy, see if you can hit him into the river," he would say. After due deliberation Tav would oblige. And I would say, "Thanks a bunch, Both." Tavaré knew my limitations as a bowler; he had seen me starting out at university. Once the damp ball had been returned, Chris permitted himself a little smile in my direction.

At county level Tavaré frequently belied his reputation. He could tear attacks apart. This was more likely to happen in one-day cricket when he would gently advance down the pitch, head still, bat raised, the ominous precursor to him smashing the ball as hard as anyone in the game. He could deliver the most devastating of innings, though anyone newly arrived in his dressing room would not have a clue from Tavaré's demeanour about the outcome of his latest visit to the crease. Whether he had been dismissed for nought or 150 the bat would be gently returned into a meticulously well-ordered coffin before he sat down to mull over what had just happened.

In the end we were reunited. He moved to Somerset in 1989 and played so well that, to his astonishment, he was called up for one last, unhappy Test match against the Australians. At Taunton his contributions from second slip were again invaluable to a flustered captain. Tav speaks slowly and only after careful contemplation, but he always delivered a clear and decisive answer to my pleas for guidance. He even had the temerity to suggest that I usually followed the advice of the last man I had spoken to.

It was fun to bat with him again. Not much had changed except that he had acquired a gum shield since our university days – he was never one to leave too much to chance. Hence one or two adjustments had to be made. I learnt that a muffled, low-pitch "onng onn eennn" from his end meant, "Come on, then." Fortunately he was always a good judge of a run and, I am glad to say, he would extricate the gum shield for mid-wicket conferences.

I deserted him at the end of 1989 by joining the *Observer*. Chris kept playing for Somerset – as captain – until 1993. Two decades on, cricket followers still identify the name of Tavaré immediately, albeit as the epitome of the archetypal, bloody-minded blocker of the Eighties. Those that played with him know that he was much more than that – as a batsman and a team-mate.

Enid Bakewell

Enid Bakewell

by Rachael Heyhoe Flint

Rachael Heyhoe Flint played 22 Tests and 23 one-day internationals for England (1960-82), captaining the side when it won the inaugural World Cup in 1973. She also played hockey for England. She now sits in the House of Lords as Baroness Heyhoe Flint of Wolverhampton.

Enid Bakewell played 12 Tests and 23 one-day internationals for England (1968-82). In 2014 *Wisden Cricketers' Almanack* selected her as one of the five greatest women players of all time.

Enid Bakewell became a legend in women's cricket in the 1970s, long before the days of extensive media coverage of our sport. Thus she inadvertently created for herself what is nowadays termed a high profile and has become a legendary name throughout the world of all cricket – and is still playing club cricket in her 70s!

The title of 'legend' is used too lightly in sport but, in relative terms, Enid captured that status at the age of 28 on her very first tour to Australia and New Zealand in 1968/69. She became the first player in the history of women's cricket to achieve the double. On the four-month trip she scored 1,031 runs at an average of 39.60 and took a remarkable 118 wickets with her slow left-arm spin at 9.7 per wicket. I was Enid's captain on this tour and not only was she an outstanding player she was a great entertainer both on and off the field, the life and soul of every reception, party and team meeting.

Enid came from a non-sporting family; she was born in a mining village called Newstead in Nottinghamshire, an only child. Her dad, Len, was a mine deputy and shot-firer, who worked at Newstead Colliery for 40 years on night shifts. Enid's mum, May, stayed at home to look after the family. Enid attributed her great powers of concentration while batting to her early childhood days when her father would take her to a local Workers Educational College when he was on study courses; Enid had to sit among adult students, patiently waiting for her father's lectures to end. To keep her quiet, her father set her the task of colouring in patterns on graph paper. Perhaps I should have tried giving Enid colouring exercises to keep her quiet in the England dressing room while we were trying to concentrate during tense moments in our Test matches!

Enid's dad, Len Turton, was a local councillor. He drove a WRVS van round the village even in his 80s. He was always a huge supporter of Enid's cricket and proved an invaluable help looking after her young children while she was batting and bowling for club, county and country and while her husband Colin was working long and often late hours as an instruments engineer at Rolls Royce in Hucknall.

In her childhood Enid could be described as a 'tom boy' and in her words: "There were no exciting games when I was a kid and only a few girls around who all played with dolls. When I was nine, I had a pair of football boots, and the boys and I played football – with me not showing it hurt when I got kicked. But my real love was cricket. My parents encouraged me and bought me cricket equipment and, because I had the gear, the boys used to call round home for me to have a game of cricket."

Enid's early cricket days with the boys in the street in Newstead progressed to a field alongside the vicarage. In the summer holiday when the local pit ponies were given two weeks off from pulling the colliery trucks and put to graze on the field, Enid's gang were moved on. So she and the boys literally cut themselves a cricket pitch with scissors and shears on an old disused field by the Newstead Cemetery. Enid describes it as "rough and ready".

I always reckoned that the rather unkempt nature of Enid's village pitch taught her to use her feet rather than letting the ball bounce. Adept footwork was the hallmark of her batting; she would skip down the wicket, even in her first over at the crease, regardless of the status of the game.

Enid made her county cricket debut for Nottinghamshire when she was only 14. She also played county and Midlands hockey, a tenacious defender with a great eye for the ball. That hand/eye ball skill was probably also learned batting on the rough and ready home-made cricket pitch. Enid in her early county days was an opening bat, only bowling as an after-thought. But she was coached and coaxed into taking her bowling more seriously – and modelled her action on Tony Lock, even imitating his lively bouncy rhythmic run-up with the same number of steps.

Enid didn't take life or sport too seriously. She was particularly amusing in the dressing room and also when we should have been on our best behaviour representing our country at rather formal official receptions. On the '68/69 tour of Australia and New Zealand we were kitted out with various off-the-field outfits donated by Marks & Spencer. Enid always had the ability to wear the wrong outfit, even though we had team meetings the day before to plan our wearing apparel (and occasionally our tactics!). She would turn up in a white blouse with red skirt and blue blazer, even though everyone else was wearing the blue-spotted white blouse or tracksuits. Or she would wear our nice little crimplene M&S cocktail dress when the rest of us wore blazers and skirts!

At most of our official receptions and parties on tour, alcohol would be served. Nothing unusual there – but Enid's father was a Methodist and so she had never been a drinker of anything stronger than fruit juice. But on tour, in order to be polite, Enid would sip the occasional sherry. Sometimes she would put on a Scottish accent. I think that's when I dubbed her with the nickname of Aggie – which to me sounded like a house-keeper character from *Dr Finlay's Casebook*, the very popular TV Scottish doctor's series. And she is still Aggie to me almost 60 years later!

I fleetingly became aware of Enid and her devil-may-care approach to sport when I played county cricket and hockey for Staffordshire against

Nottinghamshire. I got to know her much better when she was a fellow student at Dartford College of Physical Education, albeit two years below me, in 1960. Dartford was well known for producing England cricketers (and PE teachers) with our lecturers including Mary Duggan and Ruth Westbrook, captain and wicket-keeper of England in the late '50s and '60s. As college captain I was blessed with team members who all went on to represent England: Mary Pilling, Jackie Elledge, Mollie Hunt, Ann Jago, Sandra Brown – and, of course, Enid.

Enid's England career meant many sacrifices, mainly family and financial ones, and also demonstrated her strength of character in overcoming these difficulties. She married Colin in 1964, and her first daughter Lorna was born in 1966, so she missed our home series against New Zealand. But she was determined to keep fit for future tours by running with baby Lorna in the pram the two miles to visit her mother! Then came her most difficult decision when she was named in the 1968 squad of 16 for the Australasian tour. This was a four-month tour – but Enid's family, mother, father and husband Colin convinced Enid that Lorna would miss her more when she was older than at two-and-a-half. This must have been a tough choice for Enid. In those days there was no instant social media or skyping communication – but only occasional, very short and expensive phone calls home and the anxious wait for air mail letters to come from England. They took about a week to ten days to catch up with us.

All of the players on this tour, true amateurs, had to raise money to fund travel expenses – almost £650. Enid reached her target by selling chocolate and second-hand books, and setting up a fruit-and-veg stall on the road side in her village, which she stocked from her dad's allotment. Even to this day Enid loves her gardening, and she works with her son Robert on his allotment – he lives nearby in Newstead. "I like to help with his digging," she tells me, "so that I still have the strength to lift my Gunn and Moore bat."

Enid's first personal 'sponsorship in kind' came as a result of her high sporting profile in her native county after her triumphs Down Under in '68/69. Reg Simpson, the Nottinghamshire and England legend who represented Gunn and Moore, saw a photo of Enid wielding a rather ancient version of one of their bats, held together with black adhesive tape. Reg invited Enid to visit Gunn and Moore's showroom and choose a new bat. Thus began a very happy sponsorship partnership.

Enid's performances on that 1968/69 Australasian tour were so outstanding that she became the first woman cricketer – after 75 years of women's Test cricket – to be featured in *Wisden*, a five-page spread no less. Her achievements are impressive to read, even 45 years on. In Adelaide she opened with a century in her first ever Test innings, when her devastating footwork proved too much for the Australian bowlers. She took five wickets in an innings on twelve occasions on the tour. A second Test century versus New Zealand in Wellington was followed by a third in Christchurch.

Additions to Enid and Colin's family, with the births of Lynne in 1970 and Robert in 1971, prevented Enid going on two tours of the West Indies. Both were sponsored by 'Union Jack' – Sir Jack Hayward. He was born in my home town of Wolverhampton and amazingly answered a begging letter from me late in '69 after we penniless, amateur women cricketers desperately needed financial backing to send an England team to Jamaica. Sir Jack agreed to sponsor our sport in any way possible – because "I love women and I love cricket and I've read about you all in the *Daily* and *Sunday Telegraph*."

NB: 'A Special Correspondent' for the *Telegraph* sports pages was one Rachael Heyhoe. Enid recalled how, after a day's play, I would send all the details back to Fleet Street – transfer-charge telephone calls, no laptops invented then – but it paid off with Sir Jack!

It was Sir Jack's idea, with his sponsorship, to stage the first ever women's World Cup of Cricket in 1973. The first men's World Cup was not until 1975. This tournament of seven teams gave Enid another stage to show off her talents, although 'showing off' was never one of Enid's traits. She has always been refreshingly modest, attributing her bowling achievements in '68/69 to the skill of her wicket-keeper Shirley Hodges who made 13 stumpings off Enid's beguilingly tempting bowling. She certainly gave the ball plenty of air!

Back to the 1973 World Cup. In England's first match, versus an International XI at Hove, Enid and fellow opener Lynne Thomas both scored unbeaten centuries in an opening stand of 246, a world record that would last 25 years. Enid was also Player of the Match when England won the final at Edgbaston versus Australia in the presence of HRH Princess Anne. Vivian Jenkins in the *Sunday Times* wrote: "Enid Bakewell, mother of three, was England's prop and stay in the final and decisive match. She scored 118 out of England's 279-3 in the 60 overs."

In 1976 in the home series against Australia, Enid and Lynne were at it again. In the Second Test at Edgbaston they had a century stand in both innings: 116 and 164. Such was Enid's respect for Lynne throughout their Test match careers that Enid named her second daughter Lynne after her Welsh-born friend.

Apart from always putting on her left sock first, Enid was always amazingly calm and level-headed. I asked Lynne Thomas about opening with her, and she agreed:

> Enid was brilliant to open with. She was – or gave the impression of being – so calm and matter-of-fact. Walking out to the middle she would say, 'We know what we have to do so let's just go and do it.' She never mentioned the word 'try'. She was so positive you felt as if you were in full control of the situation from the moment you stepped onto the field. When we got to the middle, she would say, 'Good luck, see you lunch time' or 'tea time'. I always felt I would still be there to walk off with her.
>
> I thought her calling and running between the wickets was good. I felt confident we would make it every time. I remember her telling me to call anything going through point and backward of point as I could see the angle better when facing, better than she could as the one backing up. She had moments of talking a lot, mainly *at* the opposition!! I remember telling her to shut up at one time for me to concentrate.
>
> She controlled our batting. She would say, 'We are doing OK, just carry on the way we are' or 'We need to push for a few singles to bring the field in, then we can hit through them.'
>
> She was great to open with, and I loved it. We just seemed to hit it off on the field – and are still great friends and often travel together to cricket at home and abroad.

Enid and Lynne – who else? – opened in the historic first ever Women's match at Lord's in 1976, the culmination of the Australians' tour. The one-day match gathered huge media coverage – with the women breaking down the 'men-only' barrier for the first time since cricket started at the ground in 1814. The dynamic duo managed another top partnership of 85 as England beat Australia by eight wickets. Lynne was out first for a 'modest' 30; Enid managed 50 before being run out in a mix-up with Chris Watmough.

She left the field to a standing ovation and with a smile on her face, which at the time, as I passed her on the way out to bat, I put down to her unfailing cheerfulness. In fact, she told me recently that she got herself out on purpose: "Chris Watmough told me off, but I thought you had done so much to get us to play at Lord's that you would want to bat." Too right I did – but not at the expense of her having the chance to score a century on such a high-profile occasion!

Enid's final Test series was against the West Indies in 1979 – marked by a century and two fifties to top the averages with a mere 103.00.

Combining motherhood and cricket was rarely a hindrance to Enid with her family support – although there were occasional strains between her and husband Colin. Enid was once asked to play for a local village men's team during pit holidays which had made them a few players short. Colin told Enid if she played, he would leave home. She played, and Colin packed his suitcase and left for the night!

Impending motherhood the first time round did not deter Enid – and in 1966, at seven months pregnant, she was still playing club cricket. She stopped only because she was forced by 'health and safety regulations'.

Enid enjoys her family life. Lorna is a chartered accountant living in Cheshire; Lynne is a physiotherapist – with a five-year-old son Sam, with whom Grandmother Enid plays football: "He always wants to win – cannot think where he learned that!" Her son, Robert, is an accountant and lives in his grandfather's house in Newstead; often, with his sister – MCC member Lorna – he accompanies Enid to Lord's where she is an Honorary Life Member.

Advancing middle age proved no problem for Enid. She played in the 1982 World Cup in New Zealand, aged 41 – the end of her international career – but her reluctant retirement marked the beginning of Enid "putting something back into the sport I love". Even in her 70s she has played club cricket for the Surrey club Redoubtables – "bowled nine overs; wear little wicket-keepers pads for batting – lighter when running between the wickets. I have, of course, played for the MCC women – even played last year *[2015]* on the Nursery Ground."

Enid's heart has always dwelt in Nottinghamshire, and she has a strong affiliation to Trent Bridge where in her early international days she would practise each Sunday with the county players – "while my dad cooked Sunday lunch for the family". The Notts captain Mike Smedley said that on merit Enid could easily have played county 2nd XI cricket and not been out of place. I'm sure the men would have enjoyed Enid's lively competitive company as well.

Enid has the top coaching award, gained at Trent Bridge; it used to be called the MCC Advanced Coaching Certificate. She has served as Young England Coach/Manager, England senior selector and even now in her 70s she coaches a local girls' team called Portland CC.

Even with all Enid's amazing achievements in cricket, she is one of the most modest, unassuming people you could wish to meet. Honours and awards have been heaped on her: ECB's Lifetime Achievement Award,

MCC honorary life membership, induction into ICC's Hall of Fame in 2012, and her latest in 2015 the *Sky/Sunday Times* Lifetime Achievement.

At the ICC Hall of Fame induction in Colombo, Sri Lanka, Enid shared the stage with fellow inductee Brian Lara – or perhaps I should say Brian Lara shared the stage with Enid. She took over the microphone without ceremony or invitation and had the prestigious cricket audience of hundreds in absolute stitches with some of her off-beat anecdotes.

"I wanted to stop the interviewer asking the same boring questions about the difference between men's and women's cricket. I was also very sorry not to meet Glenn McGrath and Shane Warne, who were also inductees but did not turn up."

In the *Sky/Sunday Times* Lifetime Achievement on television, she dissolved the audience with her final quip of the supposedly serious interview by saying "Lifetime Achievement – but it's a bit early, isn't it?" The love affair between Enid and cricket, even at the age of 75, isn't over yet.

Portland CC, the club where she now coaches, is based at Nuncargate, Harold Larwood's first club in the village where he spent his childhood. "The other day," Enid told me, "I delivered a Labour Party leaflet to the house in Kirkby Woodhouse where Larwood later lived."

This is the only time I would disagree with my cricket mate. She was delivering a Labour Party leaflet, and my affiliation in the House of Lords is to the Conservatives. But Enid is the sort or person with whom you would find it very difficult to fall out.

Enid's modesty shines through. She told me about the three famous statues in Kirkby-in-Ashfield, the nearest town to Nuncargate: a bronze statue of Larwood in full flow, running up between Morrison's supermarket and the public library; fielding at silly mid off is Bill Voce, Larwood's Notts and England team-mate. Don Bradman, in baggy bronze cap, is about 22 yards away.

"And where are you, Enid?" I asked. "You are just as famous."

"As usual women play second fiddle. I am on the brick wall at the back of a Plaza where the local council hope to stage events. There are several shots of me batting – somewhat obscured by the dirt from the elements!"

Surely Enid deserves a bronze statue, to stand proudly among such cricketing legends!

Goodness knows what Enid will next achieve – probably the first woman to play cricket on the moon! Nothing will surprise me with Enid – but I am proud to say she has been a wonderful friend, supporter and the greatest Team Mate!

Zaheer Abbas

by Alastair Hignell

Alastair Hignell played cricket for Cambridge University (1975-78), and Gloucestershire (1974-83). A rugby union full back, he was capped 14 times by England. He spent many years in broadcasting and is now Patron of Multiple Sclerosis UK, a disease with which he was diagnosed in 1999.

Zaheer Abbas played cricket for Pakistan International Airways (1969-87), Gloucestershire (1972-85) and Pakistan (78 Tests, 1969-86, 14 as captain). He is now President of the International Cricket Council.

Zaheer Abbas

Dorset had Cerne Abbas, Hampshire had Itchen Abbas. Gloucestershire had the best Abbas of all. Zaheer Abbas. A man called Zed ... my team-mate.

He sees it like a football and slaps it around like a squash ball. You see it like a squash ball and slap it around like a medicine ball. He's homing in on his second century of the match. You've just escaped your second duck. What do you say when, at a between-overs conference, the best batsman in the world seeks your help?

You say yes. Whatever the question. Even if it is "Higgy, can you speak Urdu?" – and you can't. Your first thought is: "60 million people speak it around the globe. They seem to find it easy enough." Your second is: "I've lived in Germany, been on rugby tours to France, Italy and Japan, and can say 'hallo', 'goodbye' and 'two more beers, please' in four different languages. In comparison to most other county cricketers, I'm a polyglot. How difficult can it be?"

Then you realise that Zed means here and now. Tentatively you suggest that you don't expect to be entirely fluent by the time the bowler begins his run-up in approximately 30 seconds. You are relieved that Zed only wants you to understand one word. 'Shalo'. You're told it means 'run'.

Which is a bit superfluous really, considering that your role in a partnership between the best batsman in the world at the peak of his form and a player not far off the opposite on both counts is to do just that: run. On the sixth ball of every over. The fifth if you're lucky.

Everybody on the ground knows this already. Your pads, shirt and trousers are streaked green from diving desperately at the crease with ever-decreasing margins of safety. Your elbows are bruised and your knees hurt. Never fear, Zed has come up with a cunning plan.

Another one. The first had been simple enough. "This over, Higgy, when I shout 'No', I mean 'Yes'!"

You could see the logic. "And, when you shout 'Yes'?" you ask.

He rolls his eyes in exasperation, but you feel it's important to be absolutely clear. "When I shout 'Yes', he patiently explains, "I mean 'Yes'!"

That plan rumbled, we'd moved swiftly on to hand signals. Zed would ostentatiously raise his arm when a fielder had the temerity to intercept one of his boundary-bound shots. A tiny flicker of the fingers, meant only for you, would indicate that he wanted to run anyway.

The opposition caught on quick, but Zed was ever-resourceful. "This over, Higgy, you look at my eyes." Given that he was wearing spectacles and had a perspex visor attached to his helmet, this posed more problems than expected. Which was why Zed had decided that we communicate in Urdu.

You watch four deliveries with a certain amount of complacency. For the fifth, you're on your marks. So are the fielders. A brilliant stop. Absolutely no chance of a single. Last ball of the over, real pressure. Another magnificent shot, another brilliant stop. No chance, but ... Zed has spotted a slight fumble. "Shalo ... Juld-eeeee ..." he screams and runs. Rocked back on your heels, you've no chance but, if one of us has to go ... You set off for the other end and dive more in hope than expectation. A poor throw, a wicket-keeper fumble. Somehow you're still in ... and burning with curiosity.

"Tell me, Zed," you venture, as you rub away at another streak of green and notice that the scab on your elbow has opened. "What does shalo juldee mean?"

Zed has the grace to look faintly apologetic. "Oh that," he says, "that means 'run like f——'!"

Strangely enough, you don't mind. You know that you are in the company of cricketing genius. You may be biased, but even in a county championship suffering from an embarrassment of Richards – Barry for Hampshire and Viv for Somerset were blazing their own meteoric paths – you can't imagine a better batsman. Or a more unlikely-looking one.

Bespectacled, studious and mild-mannered, Zed seemed more like a check-in clerk at Pakistan International Airways than the star player for its cricket team. Skinny, frail and allergic to strenuous exercise, he was a reluctant fielder and couldn't see the point of taking more than two paces to deliver his apologetic off-spin. He hated the cold – but not as much as compatriot Sadiq who went out to field one icy afternoon in April wearing his pyjamas under his tracksuit under his cricket whites – and he disliked the daily grind of the county cricket circuit. But boy, could he bat!

When Zaheer was at the crease, the whole thing looked ridiculously simple. Upright and elegant, he was equally at ease off front foot or back, but such were his reflexes that he quite often switched from one to the other mid-shot. Stylish and graceful, he never seemed to hurry a stroke, or offer a false one. At the top of a back-lift with more twirls than a cheerleader's baton, he seemed to pause for the fraction of a second before bringing the bat crashing down at the last moment to send the ball scorching away to the boundary. Despite the spectacles, he had the eyesight of an eagle. He also had the wrists of a squash-player. It may have looked effortless, and fluent and rhythmic and all the other adjectives that were showered on Zed's batting, but, whenever Zaheer hit a ball, it stayed hit. And such was his feel for a gap that it rarely went straight to a fielder. Zed could play defensively but couldn't see much point in doing so. Even when he seemed to be going along quietly, by his standards, it only took a glance at the scoreboard to note that the runs were still flowing freely.

Zaheer loved to bat. When he got to the crease, Zed entered a world of his own where all that mattered was the bat in his hands and the possibilities it offered. He never set out to dominate the opposition. All he wanted to do was bat for as long as possible – and score runs – which to Zed was one and the same thing. If in the process records were broken, that was as it should be. If bowlers' hearts were broken as well, that was collateral damage.

They dubbed him the Asian Bradman and, like the Don, Zed dealt in big scores. Four of his 12 Test centuries were doubles, including the first one – a mammoth nine-hour 274 against England at Edgbaston in only his second Test – as well as the one that made him the first batsman from the sub-continent to hit a hundred hundreds. That was his second double century against India, the first coming at the end of a then world record of 583 runs in a three-match series.

He also hit a second double-century against England: 240 at the Oval on Pakistan's 1974 tour. By then he had been capped by Gloucestershire, most of whose batting records looked unassailable in the hands of all-time greats WG Grace and Wally Hammond. But, while neither of those managed a double-century and a hundred in the same match, Zaheer managed it FOUR times. In all eight innings he was unbeaten. And county championship matches only lasted three days in the late '70s and early '80s. And there was a 100-over limit on each first innings. And he didn't open the innings.

But these were not just one-offs. In 1976, apart from the 230 not out and 104 not out against Kent and the 216 not out and 156 not out against Surrey, he hit seven other centuries and topped the national averages with 2,431 runs. In 1981, the year of his 215 not out and 150 not out against Somerset, he didn't bat in May, scored 1,000 runs in June, 2,230 all season, and only saw his average drop below 100 in the last stages of the campaign. In 206 matches for Gloucestershire he scored over 16,000 runs at an average of 49.79.

As a team-mate for the best part of ten years, I watched him score most of those runs and I was lucky enough to witness many of them from the other end. I like to think that by the end of the decade we were on a perfect wavelength. I knew better than to ask him for advice about how the wicket was playing or what particular bowlers were doing. "If I tell you," he said, "you'll only start worrying, and you've got enough problems as it is!"

It's not that they broke the mould when they made Zed, just that he was uncopiable. As with all geniuses, he didn't always know why he played certain shots. Sometimes he didn't seem to know how he played them. From 22 yards away I would notice that, as the bowler delivered, he would change his grip on the bat-handle ... sometimes gripping lightly at the top to exaggerate the whip-crack of some of his strokes ... sometimes grasping fiercely at the bottom of the blade with his right hand to increase the bludgeoning power. I would ask why he made this or that alteration. He couldn't explain it. It was, I suppose, the difference between bat as rapier and bat as sabre.

What never changed, however, was his love of batting and his single-minded concentration on it. He also had had an obsession with setting records which, as team-mates, we were only too happy to feed. While one of us would lavish praise on another great innings, someone else would chip in with a "of course, Wally ..." or "mind you, when WG ...". Zed's jaw would set, and we'd settle happily back to watch him re-write another page in the Gloucestershire record book.

And sometimes we'd do our bit as well. After his double century at Canterbury, Zed was closing in on a second-innings hundred when a flurry of wickets and some parsimonious bowling from Derek Underwood put not only that milestone but the chance of a Gloucestershire victory in doubt. I went out to bat with captain Tony Brown's words ringing in my ears. "If you see one you like the look of, Higgy, give it a belt ...!" I looked at Deadly's 7-2 off-side field and realised that, even if I possessed a cover-drive, or any kind of off-side game come to that, I'd be unlikely to score on that side of the wicket.

I mowed, I paddled, I hacked in increasingly ugly desperation. I connected once. Tony Brown and the guys in the dressing room cheered. I hacked again. They whooped. Zed came down the wicket. I thought he was going to congratulate me. "From now on, Higgy, you block."

I looked at the scoreboard, which now indicated that only if Zed scored 19 of the last 20 or so we needed for victory would he reach his hundred. "Trust me," he said. I blocked. The dressing room groaned. Kent sensed an unlikely draw. 'Deadly' turned the screw. I blocked. The number of remaining deliveries dwindled. Zed manoeuvred the strike and then, as if shelling peas, threaded the ball through one off-side gap after another after another. Job done.

I also learnt that he really was as shy and as unassuming as he looked when he asked me to help him write letters to potential benefactors in his testimonial year. Knowing that he was as reluctant to turn out in benefit matches as he was to make personal appearances, I asked him how he proposed to secure some of their largesse. "Just say I am the best batsman in the world. That should be good enough."

That was something about which his team-mates never had the slightest doubt. On his day – and there were so many of those – Zed was as unstoppable as he was insatiable. Sometimes we got the impression the opposition was bowling for run-outs – quite often mine. I usually went if not willingly, then philosophically.

Only once did I venture a comment. After one complete mash-up of yes-no, hand signal, wink and an anguished "Shalo juldee ...!", I found myself at the same end as Zed. He was in. I was out. Again. I couldn't resist a parting comment. "Tell you what, Zed, from now on, why don't we just juldee this for a game of soldiers?"

Stephen Isted

Stephen Isted

by Michael Simkins

Michael Simkins is an actor who founded the Harry Baldwin Occasionals, a wandering cricket club in Sussex. He wrote of his lifelong obsession with the game and of the exploits of the Baldwins in the best-selling book *Fatty Batter*.

Stephen Isted is a fellow Baldwin. He works for the National Health Service.

It was Margaret Thatcher who averred – somewhat unwisely in view of subsequent satire – 'Every Prime Minister needs a Willie.' She was, of course, referring to Tory grandee and staunch supporter William Whitelaw, a politician whose loyalty and unflappability was only matched by his ability to get things done, often against insuperable odds. Well, as captain and progenitor of the Harry Baldwin Occasionals, the ultimate Sunday social team, my cricketing version of Mrs Thatcher's dictum would be 'Every cricket team needs a Stevie.' I refer, of course, to Stephen Isted.

The Baldwins, a team created by yours truly in 1984 in a desperate attempt to buttress my love of sociable cricket against its worst excesses – over-competitiveness, opprobrium for any team member who dropped a catch or missed a stumping, and a humour bypass once the coin was tossed – had been going about three years when this genial Colossus showed up on my radar.

I'd first come across Isted playing against us – for a local side named Worthing Chippingdales, if memory serves me – and, spotting his genuine cricketing credentials, at once set myself the task of trying to poach him from their bosom to buttress our own far flimsier cricketing décolletage. It is an inviolate law of Sunday social cricket that possession is nine-tenths of ownership and that decent players without a full dance card are fair game.

And so it transpired that a few weeks later, with 'the Chipps' having a Sunday off, and with us playing against a team of more ability and less substantial waistlines than ourselves, the Baldwins managed to secure Isted's services for one game only. He even arrived with his own kit, a rare blessing in the scruffy sporting hinterland that we occupied.

Within a mere few hours he had already had his stoicism and indomitable spirit put to the severest possible test. Not that he was larruped by some batting whiz-kid for eight an over, or had been bowled first ball – far from it, he scored a fluent 27 and he had figures of 2-33 off 10 – but whilst we were fielding in the second innings, the municipal breezeblock shed that laughingly served both teams as changing rooms and pavilion had been emptied by a posse of shifty teenage louts who'd been hanging about the adjoining toilet block for much of the afternoon.

On our return we discovered everything had gone – car keys, bank cards, cash – why, they'd even taken a tube of Opal Fruits Isted had brought along to sustain him for the long hours in the field. Many a ringer would have been put off by such a dismal occurrence; and indeed, despite having plied him with shandies and crisps in the pub afterwards, we expected to see him no more.

But we'd made the mistake, as so many opposition teams were to do in the years ahead, of underestimating him; underneath this mild-mannered, portly, Clark Kent demeanour, there beat the heart and the physique of Superman. He might not get padded up in a telephone box, but in other ways here was a true comic book hero. Something in Isted had spotted a kindred spirits in the Baldwins – not least a wry, Jack Bennyesque collective humour in times of strife that appealed to his own modest view of his ability. The following week his name was again on the team sheet. He was to miss hardly a game for the next two decades.

And he could turn his hand to everything. And I mean everything. He bowled left-arm fast-medium with a barrelling approach off a short run, accurate, deadly and probing – by which I mean that five times out of six he could land the ball on the cut strip. Angling the new ball across the right hander he often induced an early nick, and despite the fact that the Baldwins rarely possessed anyone in the slip cordon who could actually hang onto the darned thing, he'd merely offer a slight smile by way of disappointment at another spilled chance, before rolling up his sleeves and returning to his run-up for another tilt. Eight or ten overs were virtually de rigueur when Isted was bowling; indeed, he most closely resembled Australia's Alan Davidson and, like the legendary 'Davo', his team-mates turned to him often to staunch the runs or make the vital breakthrough.

As a batsman he was a captain's joy. With a solid defence and a pugnacious array of counter-attacking strokes, he was shunted up and down the order like some human elevator according to the needs of the team. When pressed into opening against some young speed demon, he rarely stepped away but offered doughty and resolute defence. When positioned further down the order, he fulfilled the role so often demonstrated for the West Indies by Larry Gomes – dogged retrenchment if we were 30 for four, or wristy strokeplay on the rare occasions when the pressure was off. On the exceptionally few occasions in which we were spoilt for choice, he accepted demotion to number ten or eleven without the usual surly bad grace and muttered oaths that so often accompany such disappointments in club cricket.

The only time he nearly disgraced himself was in the early 1990s when we were playing at Findon Park against a team called, I think, Worthing Railways. Coming in with only three runs needed for victory but with no more wickets to fall, Isted walked to the crease with explicit instructions from his gallant and wise commander – me – that on no account to play silly buggers but to merely push the ball around and, in the words of George

Hirst, 'get 'em in singles'. I couldn't have been clearer or more dictatorial if I'd been Mrs Thatcher herself.

But even the most loyal lieutenant has his moment of madness – just as Geoffrey Howe did – and in Isted's case, far from having his bat broken before the game by the team captain as Howe would have claimed, he committed hari-kari by his own hand, hoisting the first delivery he faced in lunatic fashion high into the air back over the bowler. It had hit only the very toe of his bat. After an agony, with the ball hanging in the air and with jubilant fielders closing in from all points of the compass, it fell just short of long on. Meanwhile Isted ran three, and we prevailed.

In fairness, due to an administrative mix-up with the kitbag, the entire match had been played with only a set of child-sized stumps at one end, and it may be that Isted reckoned he was unlikely to be bowled if he had a wild yahoo. But he damned nearly lost us the match that day, and the mood was flinty in the clubhouse for several seconds after his return. Certainly if I'd had a handbag within reach I'd have known what to do with it. But this was, as far as I can recall, his sole cricketing solecism in nearly two decades of otherwise trusty service.

This was just the start of his talent. A fine cover fielder, in motion he resembled South Africa's Colin Bland – in contrast to his fellow fielders who more usually conjured up images of Beatrix Potter's Pigling Bland. Many a slumbering batsman was duped by his apparently stout frame mooching about in the field, only to find themselves well short of their ground as he swooped to pick up and throw. Thrilling stuff.

What else? Well, he had a car – invariably an asset in social cricket – and was always happy to do innumerable pick-ups of far-flung and less mobile team-mates, often diverting from his home in Worthing to Lancing, Sompting and even Brighton before braving the hell of a summer afternoon in the traffic jams of the M23. Pub stops, the desperate cry from those in the back to empty their failing bladders, often at the same time as visiting the next pub! Isted was ever willing and uncomplaining. He knew with exquisite instinct which fellow members could afford petrol money and who couldn't.

I never once recall him being late or failing to pay his match fee. He would be the first to go and collect the boundary markers or empty the bins at close of play. He even undertook the hellish task of match managing – finding eleven players with four limbs and a head – without complaint, even though it condemned him to spending nearly all the week on the phone and having to fork out for astronomical BT bills at the end of the quarter.

So. A keen player, can do a bit in all departments, reliable, fit, has own car, stands his round in the pub. All well and good, you might think, but nothing that can't be replicated by thousands of cricketers in hundreds of teams the length and breadth of the country. But Isted had one abiding and indispensable quality, shared by few others. He was, by profession, an NHS nurse. This meant that in addition to his own merits on the field, he ensured that other protagonists around him also stayed fit and healthy during active service.

Innumerable occasions spring to mind in which his expertise and healing hands kept us in the game instead of ending our day at the local A&E. Dislocated fingers, minor sprains, head bumps, bruises: nothing was beyond his medical expertise, although few incidents were more dramatic than the occasion on which he ran from the field, mid-over, to save and resuscitate a drowning child in a nearby swimming pool.

We all put our life and livelihoods in the tender care of this modern angel of mercy, allowing him to minister to whatever ailments befell us during hours of play. It was only years later that he confessed that he was in fact a psychiatric nurse, and had no medical qualifications whatsoever beyond the most rudimentary first aid and good common sense. No matter – entire world religions have been founded on such misconceptions. At the time we believed, and had reason to be grateful.

His match stats are, as match stats always are, only mildly interesting in a desiccated sort of way. 1594 runs at 16.60, and 182 wickets at 18.26, with a handful of half centuries along the way. But these sterile figures can give no idea of the importance of the man to our continuing fortunes, especially at a time when there was precious little else in the larder. You might as well be talking about Sobers or Botham in the context of his peers.

Years on, many of us who formed the nucleus of the original Baldwin team in those heady years at the latter end of the last century have hung up our flannels and are now marooned in bath chairs, droning on about the good old days and boring rigid a younger, fitter generation of Baldwins. Quite right too. Isted has similarly succumbed to the vagaries of old age, swapping his straining cricket whites and yellowing boots for a polo shirt, C&A slacks and tales of past glories. But as his club captain for over twenty years, I will never forget the human 'Get out of Jail Free' card that was represented by Stephen Isted. Every club captain needs a Stevie. I would still trust him with my life.

Except, of course, if I ever fall ill or injured. Next time I'll seek someone who actually has a bloody clue what they're doing ...

Bryan Stott (left) and Ken Taylor

Ken Taylor

by Bryan Stott

Bryan Stott played cricket for Yorkshire (1952-63). He has now retired after many years running a plumbing and heating business. He lives in Yeadon, near Leeds.

Ken Taylor played cricket for Yorkshire (1953-68) and England (1959-64, 3 Tests). He played football for Huddersfield Town (1953-64) and studied art at Huddersfield College and the Slade School of Fine Art in London. He lives in Norfolk where he taught art for many years.

Opening the innings with Ken was a wonderful experience for me. We were good friends, we roomed together, and in the middle we were working together, not in competition. Batting is so much more enjoyable when you're on a wavelength with your partner – and opening the innings is special. You start to get your nerves, the adrenalin starts to flow, when the other team is nine wickets down, and you're waiting to get off and gather your thoughts.

We should have been rivals because Ken and I, together with Dougie Padgett, were all coming through at the same time. Yorkshire always had two, three or four people in the Test team and, when they were away, the policy was to involve us in the first eleven, either as twelfth man or playing. They shared the opportunities between the three of us. But it never felt like Ken and I were rivals because neither of us were really ambitious for ourselves in that way.

Even when I was 13 or 14 years old at grammar school, I was working in the holidays in the family plumbing and heating business, and that was always what I was going to do. Playing for England would have been smashing, but it wasn't the ultimate thing in my life. I knew that my basic technique was not flawless, and for the future I had a business to run. Ken was very much the same. He was playing football in the winter for Huddersfield, he had his art, and he was content doing all three things.

We first met when we were on opposite sides in a boys' match: Airedale and Wharfedale Schools against Huddersfield Schools. I can remember vividly playing football with a tennis ball on the outfield before the match, and this little lad – and Ken was a little lad then, younger than the rest of us – was like a terrier, tackling people, not giving in. He was going for the ball, and he was not going to give up.

In 1949 we played together in the Yorkshire Schools cricket team and in the inaugural schools match between the North of England and the South. We progressed to the schoolboy nets at Headingley, and in 1951 we started playing together in the Yorkshire second eleven; I was 16, he was 15.

Over the next few years we had occasional games in the first eleven, but the first time we were both in the Yorkshire side was in July 1954 at Neath – our first encounter with Wilf Wooller, the Glamorgan captain. Ken made his first fifty for the county, the only fifty in the match, then Freddie Trueman bowled them out cheaply on a pudding in the second innings. We only needed 68 to win, but the pitch was wet and, when I came in to bat, it was 18 for five. Led by Wooller, the Glamorgan fielders were clustered all round me, talking away. It was a daunting experience.

It was the end of the second day, the extra half hour was taken, and we came off for bad light. Wilf, though, refused to leave the field. He stayed out there, still on the field of play, and the crowd in the rugby clubhouse started shouting and bawling. Then he began to walk towards the pavilion, and the spectators followed him like an army. He stood there, with the crowd baying, and the umpires inevitably brought us out again – in light that was worse than what it had been when we came off.

It was quite an atmosphere, and it did not get any better in the rugby club bar in the evening. Whilst we were talking to Harold Williams, the Leeds United footballer, Freddie Trueman's voice suddenly carried across the room above the hubbub: "Welshmen, there wouldn't be any Welshmen if an Englishman hadn't tupped a nanny goat." I don't think Ken was with us, but Dougie Padgett, Raymond Illingworth and I all made a hasty getaway.

The next morning, when Billy Sutcliffe and I were coming out of the pavilion to bat, there was Wilf scrubbing the ball on the concrete steps. "What the bloody hell are you doing?" Billy said, and Wilf told him to bugger off. Billy took the ball to the umpires, and they just threw it back to Wilf. They didn't fancy an argument with him.

We lost a couple of wickets, and very soon heavy rain set in. It was pouring stair rods, I can remember the water running down behind my pads, but Wilf refused to come off. Eventually Don Shepherd, who was bowling, said, "Skipper, I can't hold the ball," at which point Wilf Wooller marched off the ground, and the rest of us, including the umpires, followed. That was our baptism in the ways of Wilf Wooller. It was another world from our Yorkshire second eleven games.

At that stage Ken and I were not that close. It was three years later, after I came back from National Service in 1957, when things really clicked between us. Yorkshire had not had a settled opening pair for a while, and Billy Sutcliffe gave Ken and me a chance to do it. Our second game together was at Trent Bridge, and that was the real clincher for our friendship, the moment when the key turned in the lock, when we realised we were on the same wavelength. We started to see each other as pals, both on and off the field.

We put on 122 in the first innings, 230 in the second, and we clicked with the running. Reg Simpson, the Notts captain, was making little humorous comments: "They're getting very red in the face" and so on.

We got to know each other's game. If Ken was playing back defensively, I could tell when he got into a certain position that he was going to bob it down on the on-side and take a quick single. Sometimes we didn't even call, and that would get at the opposition. Because I had anticipated his intention I would have a two- or three-yard start, and I'd be right as a bobbin – and Ken had such strength in his legs, so much muscle they were like tree trunks, that he could burst from a standing start and be off. He had long strides, too, and would be down the other end in just a few paces.

We trusted each other. There was never any selfishness. I am absolutely certain that we both took great pleasure in each other's success. It was a shared responsibility. We were beginning to make our mark, and we were confident with each other.

We helped each other with our different styles of batting. He was right-handed, I was left. At school he had had a teacher who bowled leg-breaks and googlies so he was confident playing them whereas I had difficulty picking them. In that game at Trent Bridge Notts had Bruce Dooland, the Australian, and Gamini Goonesena, both bowling leg-breaks, and Ken slaughtered them. He could pick the flight so early, get to the pitch of the ball and blast it over extra cover. It was wonderful to watch. And, of course, that made it a lot easier for me because then they would lose their length and not bowl so well.

Later in the year we were playing in a friendly golf match near Rotherham, and Brian Sellers, the Yorkshire chairman of cricket, came up to us in the clubhouse. "You two, I want a word with you," he said, and he took us into the quiet of the billiard room. "The England selectors wanted to play you in the last Test, but I told them you were too young, not ready." Then he walked away, and we just stood there, looking at each other.

We both felt that we were ready and, if we had gone together, we would have gained great strength from each other. At that point we were on the top of the wave. Ken played for England a couple of years later, but he never felt at home in the set-up. He never did find it easy to settle into a new environment.

Yorkshire demanded quick runs. Other teams rarely gave us declarations; we had a reputation, and we had to make the going ourselves. At other counties batsmen could bat all day. Brian Bolus left us to go to Nottinghamshire, where he played his own game in his own time, and he got bucket-loads of runs. It was a different world. We always had to play for the team, and our averages were nothing special.

Our best year was 1959, a golden summer in which Yorkshire won the championship for the first time for ten years. It was the whole team that won the championship, everybody contributed to the success. For me the crucial victory was at Chesterfield in early July. Ronnie Burnet, our captain, kept losing the toss, and we were always at the fag end of things. Derbyshire were also in the running for the championship, and Donald Carr, their captain, set us to score 301 in three hours.

I had been off the field injured so I could not open with Ken – and, when I did come out to bat, Donald Carr came running over. "Go back, go back," he said, shaking his head. Every time I've seen him since, he's apologised to me: "I'm sorry, Stotty, it was a big mistake." But Ken saw us home with a fantastic innings of 144, and it launched us towards the title. That was Ken at his brilliant best.

We won the championship four times in my last five years with Yorkshire, and we were so positive. We knew how to win, and we expected to win. There was a great atmosphere in the team, and we had some wonderful characters, like Don Wilson whose enthusiasm was such a breath of fresh air. But the tensions are always there in professional sport, and there is a fine line in a dressing room between calm and explosion. You could never be sure with Freddie Trueman what was going to happen next, and we had a few moments when things erupted.

Ken was one of the quieter characters, as I was. He thinks a lot, and he was uncomfortable when the atmosphere wasn't so good. If we had something to say, we would say it, and that made us a steadying influence in the team. Neither of us sought the limelight.

I had decided to retire at the end of 1963, not expecting that I would be sent on my way by an appendix operation in August, and Geoffrey Boycott became Ken's opening partner. I never found it as easy when I batted with other partners, and I know Ken felt the same. If one of us called, the other ran; we trusted each other. But Geoffrey would be weighing up his own safety. There would have been that element of selfishness that Ken and I did not have with each other, and I know Ken was run out a few times. It must have been purgatory for him.

I was so busy at work in 1964 that I never went to any of the matches that summer. I had no contact with Ken, and I didn't know when I would see him again. Then he was called up by England for the Headingley Test. He had to report to the ground for practice on the Wednesday, then go up to the Old Swan Hotel in Harrogate for the night, and on the way from the ground to the hotel he came by and knocked on our door. He just appeared, and I was so pleased to see him. It reignited our friendship, and we have stayed firm friends ever since. He's over in Norfolk, I'm still in Yorkshire, but we still meet up regularly with our wives and visit each other's homes.

Unknown to each other we both joined the Freemasons in 1962, Ken in Huddersfield, me in Otley Wharfdale, both lodges in the Province of Yorkshire West Riding. Several of the great Yorkshire side of the 1930s were members of the Craft, and I firmly believe that the basic principles of fellowship and trust that are generated within freemasonry have been the bedrock of the long friendship between Ken and me. We have both been very fortunate to receive our Jubilee certificates from our respective Provinces, in celebration of 50 years' membership of the Craft. God willing, another as yet unbroken partnership.

When I played cricket with Ken, he was somebody I knew that I could rely on, and I feel that every bit as strongly now. There is an understanding between us that we can trust each other, a deep trust. I know that he would never do anything that was in any way detrimental to me, and he knows that about me. We don't have to think about it.

Ever since we started opening the batting together, there has been a bond between us.

Rahul Dravid

by Ed Smith

Ed Smith played cricket for Cambridge University (1996-98), Kent (1996-2004), Middlesex (2005-08) and England (2003, 3 Tests). He is now a member of the *Test Match Special* commentary team and a journalist and author with a wide range of interests.

Rahul Dravid played cricket for Karnataka (1990-2012), Kent (2000) and India (1996-2012, 164 Tests, 25 as captain). He now works with India's potential Olympians and Paralympians through the Rahul Dravid Athlete Mentorship Programme.

Rahul Dravid

When Rahul Dravid walked into the dressing room of the St Lawrence ground in Canterbury on a cold spring morning, you could tell he was different from all the others. He did not swagger with cockiness or bristle with macho competitiveness. He went quietly round the room, shaking the hand of every Kent player – greeting everyone the same, from the captain to the most junior. It was not the mannered behaviour of a seasoned overseas professional; it was the natural courtesy of a real gentleman. We met a special human being first, an international cricketer second.

The cricketer was pretty good, too. Dravid joined Kent for the 2000 season, and I spent much of it at number four, coming in one after Dravid – not that he was the departing batsman very often. That meant I had some wonderful opportunities to bat alongside the player who became the highest scoring number three of all time.

What did I learn? I learnt that real toughness takes many different forms. Dravid could appear shy and slightly vulnerable off the pitch; in the middle, you sensed a depth of resilience. Many overseas players liked to set themselves apart from the county pros – as though they had to swear more loudly and clap their hands more violently to prove that international cricketers were tougher than the rest. Not Dravid. He never paraded his toughness – it emerged between the lines of his performances. Instead, he always talked about learning, about gathering new experiences – as though his cricketing education wasn't complete, as though there were many more strands of his craft to hone. His journey, you could tell, was driven by self-improvement.

One word has attached itself to Dravid wherever he has gone: gentleman. The word is often misunderstood. Gentlemanliness is not mere surface charm – the easy lightness of confident sociability. Far from it: the real gentleman doesn't run around flattering everyone in sight, he makes sure he fulfils his duties and obligations without drawing attention to himself or making a fuss. Gentlemanliness is as much about restraint as it is about appearances. Above all, a gentleman is not only courteous, he is also constant: always the same, whatever the circumstances or the company.

In that sense, Dravid is a true gentleman. Where many sportsmen flatter to deceive, Dravid runs deep. He is a man of substance, morally serious and intellectually curious. For all his understatement, he couldn't fail to convey those qualities to anyone who watched him properly.

I last bumped into Dravid late last year at a charity dinner at the Sydney Cricket Ground. He was the same as he always has been – warm, self-deprecating, curious about the lives of others. As ever, he made a point of asking about my parents – their health and happiness – although he has never met them. Family and friendship, you sense, are central to his life and his values.

In the q&a that followed his speech, one answer got close to the core of his personality. What motivated him still, after all these years and so many runs? Dravid said that, as a schoolboy, he remembered many kids who had at least as much desire to play professional cricket as he did – they attended every camp and net session, no matter what the cost or the difficulty of getting there. But you could tell – from just one ball bowled or one shot played – that they simply didn't have the talent to make it. He knew he was different. "I was given a talent to play cricket," Dravid explained. "I don't know why I was given it. But I was. I owe it to all those who wish it had been them to give of my best, every day."

What a brilliant inversion of the usual myth told by professional sportsmen: that they had unexceptional talent and made it to the top only because they worked harder. Dravid spoke the truth. Yes, he worked hard. But the hard work was driven by the desire to give full expression to a God-given talent.

On the field, what set Dravid apart was a rare combination of technical excellence, mental toughness and emotional restraint. He was restrained in celebration, just as he was restrained in disappointment – exactly as the true gentleman should be. And yet his emotional self-control co-existed with fierce competitiveness and national pride.

Dravid has single-handedly disproved the absurd argument that tantrums and yobbishness are a sign of 'how much you care' or, worse still, 'how much you want it'. Dravid was rarely outdone in terms of hunger or passion. And he was never outdone in terms of behaviour or dignity. Those twin aspects of his personality – the dignified human being and the passionate competitor – ran alongside each other, the one never allowed to interfere with the other. He knew where the boundaries were, in life and in cricket.

I am an optimist by nature. I do not think that sport is perpetually declining from some mythical golden age. But sometimes I cannot avoid the sense that a certain type of sportsman is an increasingly endangered species. I have that feeling now, as Dravid declares his innings closed. No longer will he take guard with that familiar hint of politeness, even deference. No longer will he raise his bat to the crowd as if he is genuinely thanking them for their applause – the bat tilted outwards in acknowledgement of the supporters, not just waved frantically in an orgy of personal celebration. No longer will he stand at first slip, concise and precise in his movements – a cricketer first, an athlete second. No longer will the high Dravid back-swing and meticulous footwork link this generation with the great technicians of the past.

It would be nice to argue that no cricketer is irreplaceable, that sport is defined by continuity rather than full stops, that there will soon be another Dravid, another champion cricketer of timeless steel and dignity. But I don't think there will be. I think Dravid will be remembered as the last in a great tradition of batsmen whose instincts and temperament were perfectly suited to Test match cricket. It is not an exaggeration to say that a whole strand of the game – a rich vein that runs through the game's poetic heart – departs the scene with India's greatest ever number three. Playing Twenty20 cricket won't teach anyone to become the next Rahul Dravid.

In years to come, perhaps too late, we may realise what we have lost: the civility, craft and dignity that Dravid brought to every cricket match in which he played.

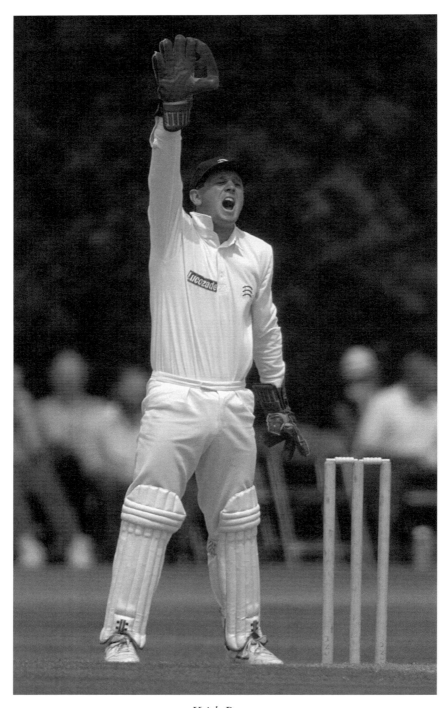

Keith Brown

Keith Brown

by Angus Fraser

Angus Fraser played cricket for Middlesex (1984-2002) and England (1989-98, 46 Tests). He is now Middlesex's Director of Cricket and an England selector.

Keith Brown played cricket for Middlesex (1984-98). He is now Head of Games at Bramdean School in Exeter.

It was not a day during which I was expecting to be surprised.

The match had been in my 2014 diary for quite a while. Many of my former Middlesex team-mates were excited by the prospect of meeting up to play one more game at Lord's. Me, if I am being totally honest – I wasn't.

It was not that the chance once again to share a dressing room, exchange stories and have a laugh with Mike Roseberry, Norman Cowans or Kevan James did not appeal to me. It was not that I didn't appreciate what an honour it is to play at cricket's most cherished ground, either.

It was just that the opportunity to try to roll back the years with the ball in my hand in front of two or three thousand people did not seem that attractive. I had accepted some time ago that the days of nipping the ball about off a good length had disappeared over the horizon. Bowling fast – or, should I say, attempting to bowl medium pace – began to hurt when I was fit and in my early thirties. Now, at 49 and with a couple of stone extra to carry around, there was only one guaranteed outcome of an afternoon in the field – several days of stiffness and pain.

In the match, between Middlesex CCC President's XI and the Marylebone Cricket Club President's XI, to commemorate the 150th and 200th anniversaries of the two great clubs, Middlesex bowled first.

Norman Cowans opened from the Nursery End but it was when Ollie Wilkin, then a member of the county's playing staff, came on to bowl, that it began to dawn on me what an under-rated and fine cricketer Keith Brown was. Ollie was recovering from injury, and this game was being used as a fitness test. He ran in hard and bowled at a lively pace, probably in the early eighties. Keith, keeping wicket for the first time in years, had looked okay against Norman's gentle medium pace, principally because very few deliveries got through to him. Ollie, I thought, would test Browny out. His extra pace and bounce were sure to cause him a few problems. I dreaded it becoming embarrassing.

How wrong I was. Keith looked as though he was still playing high-level cricket. He was magnificent. He was light on his feet, moving gracefully down the leg side to take the occasional errant delivery, and the ball entered his gloves as though it was making contact with a down-filled pillow. To say I was impressed, standing at mid-on, was something of an understatement.

As I watched Keith continue to deal skilfully with everything that was, literally, thrown his way, I began to reminisce about all the days and evenings we had spent playing cricket and socialising together in the '80s and '90s. Suddenly I realised how much I had enjoyed his company and how much we had taken his cricket skills for granted. This was a bloke, aged 50 and not having kept wicket for years, moving and catching the ball as well as some of the glovemen I regularly watch playing county cricket. It was lovely to see.

To those of us that played for Middlesex during the '80s and '90s Keith was our steady eddy. He scored important runs when we were in the mire, but they never came in a flashy, headline-grabbing manner. Such performances had earned him the nickname 'Stalwart'. In a county team that regularly contained a number of international cricketers, it was probably inevitable that the week-in, week-out, under-the-radar achievements of an 'unglamorous' player failed to catch people's attention.

Browny was born in Edmonton in north London in 1963. He has a younger brother, Gary, who was on the Middlesex playing staff in the 1980s, too. The pair were completely different characters. Keith got married young, to Marie, and was happy with a quiet life. A night out for him was a couple of pints and a bowl of peanuts at the hotel bar on an away trip. Gary was a far more sociable animal and moved up to Durham to further his career. He still lives in the north-east.

Keith came from a working-class background and, unsurprisingly, his socialist views didn't get much support in the Middlesex dressing room. Harry Sharp, our scorer, used to get in animated debates about politics with Keith, and it wasn't until Mark Ramprakash arrived at the club that he found an ally to take on the right-of-centre views of Sharp, Mike Gatting and John Emburey.

Keith played his early cricket at Edmonton before being told to move to Enfield, a stronger club that played in the Middlesex County Cricket League. Even though he went on to become Middlesex's wicket-keeper the club signed him from the MCC Groundstaff – Young Cricketers now – as a batsman.

We spent a lot of time together playing 2nd XI cricket in the mid-'80s, turning up to develop our game at places like Hinckley, Southend, Dover, Harefield and Harrow. As I look back at those days whilst writing this piece I do so with a smile on my face. They weren't the places we wanted to be playing at, but Middlesex had an outstanding team at the time and the only 1st XI chances we got were when Gatting, Emburey, Paul Downton and Cowans were away on Test duty.

We loved what we were doing and appreciated how lucky we were. The lack of opportunities frustrated us, but we had two options: (1) leave for a club where opportunities were greater, as Colin Metson, Graham Rose, Chris Lewis, Phillip DeFreitas and Kevan James did, or (2) stay behind, work hard, get better and make the most of the chance when it came along. We both chose the latter, and neither of us ever regretted it.

And, boy, did we have some fun, initially on the 2nd XI circuit staying in modest hotels, eating so-so food and occasionally attempting to avoid being caught coming in late from a dodgy nightclub by Don Bennett, our strict and highly respected coach. This is not the existence I expect from Middlesex's young cricketers now, but back then it was how it was.

Club games were fierce, especially those between my side, Stanmore, and Enfield. In one highly competitive match at Enfield I hit Browny under the chin with a bouncer. He had a nasty gash that later required stitches. On seeing blood I went down to see how he was. With industrial language and a wave of his hand he told me where to go before being patched up so that he could carry on batting. Having done quite a bit of boxing when he was young, Keith was used to a bit of blood and there was no way he was going to 'retire hurt' against me. He would have never heard the end of it.

That was one of the reasons why everyone on the Middlesex staff had so much affection for Keith. He was without doubt our toughest cricketer. He regularly played with broken fingers and pulled muscles. Having worked so hard to secure his place in the 1st XI, he wasn't going to give someone the chance to take it away because of minor ailments like those.

Browny made his Middlesex debut against Hampshire in 1984, but it was in August 1985 against the touring Australians that he highlighted his potential. In only his fourth first-class game he scored 102 against an attack that contained Craig McDermott, Geoff Lawson and Jeff Thomson. These days such a performance from a young cricketer would get people talking about an England future, but Keith started the next season back in the 2nd XI.

Clive Radley was his hero. Browny loved Rad, and he used to hang on every word he said to him. Keith loved the way Rad batted, and he played like him, too. They both loved scoring ugly runs. The uglier the better, because they knew it would wind up the opposition even more. Like Rad he scampered between the wickets, pinching singles and turning ones into twos. His technique was different. Keith, how shall I say this, favoured the leg side. Basically he shovelled everything off the stumps through the leg side. A first-class batting average of 35 shows it was highly effective but, when he was out of form, he used to get out lbw a lot. When Browny went through one of these periods, Gatting – who had a view on everything; still does – and the coaches used to say it was because his head was falling over to the off-side, a flaw that often results in a batsman playing round his front pad.

To correct this Don Bennett would have several sessions throwing balls at Keith in the nets, working on keeping his head up. After a while Bennett would tell him his head was okay, and off Keith would go scoring more runs. The fact that his head was in exactly the same position as it was before was irrelevant. The sessions had brought back his confidence.

It was only when Keith began keeping wicket that he truly established himself as a 1st XI player. Before then, between 1984 and 1991, Keith played as a top-order batsman and a fearless, and exceptionally good, short-leg. Fielding in such a position is pretty dangerous, even when skilful spinners like John Emburey and Philip Tufnell were bowling, but Browny's bravery and athleticism allowed him to take many of his 446 catches standing three yards from the bat. Such was his value that Middlesex paid him danger money to field there. Tufnell reckoned Browny's catching won him several Test caps and England tours. In appreciation of his efforts he used to buy Browny a nice bottle of scotch at the end of each season.

Once Keith got behind the stumps there was no looking back. In seven seasons he took over 300 catches and 33 stumpings. At one time, in the mid-'90s, when Alec Stewart was struggling, there were mentions of Keith and an England cap but, sadly, it never materialised.

I can't remember any of the six wickets he took, even though he used continually to remind us of them. How his horrible medium pace allowed him to take 2-7 in three overs against Gloucestershire, I will never know. Mark Alleyne and Paul Romaines must have nightmares about that day.

What I do remember are the hours of fun we had together and the occasional cracking line he produced. One took place on a pre-season tour to Portugal in the '90s. A largish group of us went for a meal at a restaurant, had a few drinks and, as they occasionally do in that part of the world, got stuck into complimentary bottles of port and brandy which the hosts had put on our table. Emburey had a couple of ports, a drink he has an allergy to, and had quite a bad reaction when we got back to the complex.

Browny had gone to his room by then but next morning, when warming up, Keith asked: "Where's Embers?" Our physio, Simon Shepherd, said: "He's not well, he has an allergy to fortified wines." Browny half-heard Simon's response, and his reaction will live with me until I leave this planet. "Forty-five wines?" he said. "No bloody wonder the pisshead's not well. That's bloody disgraceful."

Browny retired in 1998 to move down to Devon to teach sport at a junior school. I always felt he would be a good coach because of the way he dealt with people, and the fact he has such high standards and values. Sadly Middlesex's young cricketers will not benefit from working with Keith, but he is one of the greatest men I had the privilege of playing with – and one of Middlesex's finest cricketers.

Eddie Barlow

Eddie Barlow

by Geoff Miller

Geoff Miller played cricket for Derbyshire (1973-90), Essex (1987-89) and England (34 Tests, 1976-84). He was an England selector from 2000 to 2013, serving as National Selector from 2008.

Eddie Barlow played cricket for four South African states (1959-83), Derbyshire (1976-78) and South Africa (30 Tests, 1961-70). He was the national coach of Bangladesh when in 2000 he suffered a severe stroke. He died in 2005.

My love of cricket was orchestrated by a conversation with my father, who coincidentally was named Keith. Keith Miller. How could my life follow any other career path than cricket? It was obviously meant to be!

The time was 5.00am. The date was January 10, 1959.

He was preparing the fire for another freezing day in Chesterfield, listening to the radio. Australia v England in Sydney. Fred Trueman bowling to Norman O'Neill. He suggested that it would be wonderful, one day, to be listening to a commentator describing me walking out to bat for England in Australia.

The story began. I just had to grant him his wish!

Norman Vickers, a cricket fanatic five houses down the cul-de-sac where we lived, taught me the basic fundamentals of the game. Grip, stance and movement with the bat. Run up, action, accuracy with the ball.

Jim Brailsford, an ex-county cricketer with Derbyshire, took on my development when I joined Chesterfield Cricket Club. His advice and coaching significantly helped my career towards county cricket.

Then, during my early years at Derbyshire, the man who transformed my career, by explaining the requirements for becoming an international cricketer, joined the county.

Eddie Barlow arrived! He very quickly became captain of Derbyshire. He was housed in Chesterfield so we spent a lot of time together, both socially and travelling to home games – Derby, Ilkeston, Buxton, Burton – and away games all over the country. Fascinating conversations about all aspects of the game. A rapid learning process.

He gave me added responsibility on the field, with both bat and ball, but insisted that I had to respond with results. Bat higher up the order, spending more time at the crease, and bowl for longer spells, naturally with justification for the side.

He would regularly ask me, "What would you do now?", continually insisting I captained the game in my own mind. "It is how you learn the game." I definitely had to have a response!

He taught me the art of slip fielding, so we spent many hours stood together, discussing passages of play.

He had a superb positive outlook on all situations and transformed a young, mediocre county side, containing many inexperienced players, including myself, into a team that believed in itself and rapidly improved.

Eddie also recognised the 'need for fitness', which never seemed to be a significant necessity at that time, and would never tolerate a 'neglect of effort' towards being 'fit to focus'. All his own words.

Training sessions, strength and conditioning, speed work and distance running, were all part of his personal life, so naturally we had to follow suit.

Again, in his South African dialogue, "A physically fit cricketer will be able to concentrate for longer periods, which is an absolute must in the professional game ... especially in the international arena."

"Three-day cricket is a long time. Five-day Test matches are significantly longer and a challenge to the technical, physical and mental attributes of a player. ... Endurance is paramount."

I think his attitude to the game was years ahead of his time. The number of times I saw the opposition in fits of laughter, watching us preparing for a day's play by standing as a unit, on the outfield, loosening, stretching, sprinting etc. "Don't be drawn," he used to shout. "The other teams will very soon realise the error of their ways and adopt the same policy." How right he was!

I feel that all aspects of present-day cricket, certainly in relation to preparation, determination and professionalism, were entrenched in the mind of Eddie Barlow.

He would have coped naturally with the rigorous nature of the modern game, in all its forms – mentally, physically and technically.

Unfortunately the world never saw the full career of Edgar John Barlow, due to the isolation of South Africa from Test cricket. If they had, they would have seen an extremely motivated, positive, all-round cricketer, whose talent was certainly not confined to the field of play. A special individual who always played for the team.

I had the great fortune to have some wonderful mentors during my cricketing career, and I have no doubt that without the friendship, help and advice from Eddie Barlow, both on and off the field, my path would have taken a significantly different direction.

Proudly my father did listen to me walking out to bat in Sydney, with the crown and lions on my chest.

Thank you, Eddie, for making that possible.

You had some trying times towards the latter part of your life but, as ever, never gave up, always being prepared to offer advice on our only-too-rare meetings.

The modern cricketing world owes you a great debt of gratitude. Your ideas are now commonplace in all types of professional cricket.

I, for one, will never forget that.

Edgar John Barlow ... R.I.P.

John Lever

John Lever

by Derek Pringle

Derek Pringle played cricket for Cambridge University (1979-82), Essex (1978-93) and England (1982-92, 30 Tests). He has been the cricket correspondent of *The Independent* and *Daily Telegraph*.

John Lever played cricket for Essex (1967-89) and England (1976-86, 21 Tests). He now coaches at Bancroft's School in Woodford Green, Essex.

Only once did his Essex team-mates round on John Kenneth Lever. Oh, how we swore and cursed JK that early summer's day, damning the very existence of this consummate professional and dedicated team man.

We fulminated with good, if selfish, reason, our ire burning deep into the post-tea session of our county championship match against Hampshire in 1984.

For those with sharp memories, that was the season the Test and County Cricket Board decided a day's play in the championship would comprise 117 overs – one of several barmy diktats they hoped might make three-day cricket more palatable to the public. As we pushed to inflict further damage on a Hampshire side shorn of its West Indian stars Malcolm Marshall and Gordon Greenidge after making them follow on, it was natural for Graham Gooch, deputising as captain for Keith Fletcher, to turn to JK to deliver the telling blow.

The trouble was JK had a 35-yard run-up, which did not include his expansive follow-through. Usually, and this was due mostly to our creative scorer, Clem Driver, who fiddled over-rates so that we avoided fines, we rarely noticed how long JK's overs took. But that season the TCCB had dispensed with fines and teams had to bowl the overs instead, which turned chop-chop into tick-tock and our very own Orwellian nightmare.

With the pavilion clock at Northlands Road pushing 7.30pm on that evening, and with 15 overs still remaining and little prospect of bad light hastening an early bath, a collective plea broke out – "GO OFF YOUR SHORT RUN, JK." It was only after he ignored us that the air turned blue, our collective disquiet proving Bob Marley's dictum that 'hungry men are angry men.'

If the 117-overs-a-day proved an unpopular, short-lived experiment, there was nothing fleeting about the influence JK Lever exerted on Essex's fortunes. From the late 1960s, when he joined the staff as a teenager, until his retirement in 1989 at the age of 40, few players have given so unstintingly to a single cause. Loyal, companionable, generous, calm, unflagging, funny and highly talented, he was the team-mate every county wished they'd had. But he was Essex shot through, and in those days diehards like him did not stray.

We were blessed to have him and while the wickets he took for Essex with his medium-fast swingers can be measured, 2,396 across all first-team formats, what cannot be calculated is the psychological well-being felt by the team whenever JK was in it. Aside from the potency he provided with the ball, his cheery attitude and gentle wisdom were like a comfort blanket and Essex were more prone to the jitters without him. Thankfully, that was not often, his fitness record being as reliably robust as his bowling.

It is easier to play the game with a smile when you are supremely good at it, and JK rarely failed to see the fun however taut the situation. While others would eff and blind in anger or frustration, the worst he would come up with when annoyed by poor fielding or ropey umpiring was a quick shake of the head and, occasionally, an audible exhalation of breath. Otherwise, it was back to his mark in the deep blue yonder and then, with that pitter patter of steps which gradually lengthened into an athlete's stride and the rhythm swing bowlers need to get the ball moving sideways, he'd chalk up another of the 112,000-odd deliveries he sent down for Essex.

That swing, mostly in to right-handers but also, with a subtle repositioning of the shine and wrist angle, away from them as well, was the main source of his potency. That, and the ability to bowl at least three telling spells a day with scarcely a reduction in pace, were his forte.

Bowling is really a game of geometry. For those of left-arm persuasion like JK, swinging the ball back into right-handers achieves the perfect alignment for lbws under the Laws.

When left-armers start hooping it any batsman not confident of playing the ball late, especially with the movement of their feet, becomes a nervous nellie. When he got it right, which was most of the time, JK's curves possessed a Pythagorean purity and umpires' fingers loosened as a result. JK always joked that he got far more lbws than he probably deserved, and maybe he did, but few begrudged him them, even the departing batsman.

He worked the umpires too, not in the aggressive, cynical way Shane Warne used to do, but through politeness. Most in the county game thought JK a gent and umpires, former players almost to a man back then, were no exception. While the rest of us would have our run-ins with white-coated authority, JK would be all charm and smiles and the lbws racked up accordingly. You'd have thought that we might have learnt from his example but he seemed always to compete with a calmness that eluded the rest of us.

The player considered the 'captain's dream' exists mostly in the minds of fantasists, yet JK managed to embody it for Essex. Whatever the situation on the field, Keith Fletcher, or Graham Gooch, his successor as Essex captain, could rely on him to provide high-quality bowling irrespective of circumstance.

Need a wicket, whistle up JK. Need to keep it tight for 40 minutes, bring on JK. Need some yorkers at the death, give the ball to JK. He was a bowling everyman with the stamina to match. On the rare occasions Ray East or John Childs were injured or not picked, he'd even turn his hand to left-arm spin, though, it has to be said, not very well.

When not in spin mode he rarely failed to deliver, especially when the pressure was on. I say rarely. There was the occasion at Lord's in the 1989 Benson & Hedges Cup final where his failure to supply the perfect yorker cost Essex the match, when Nottinghamshire required four runs to win off the last ball.

Few will realise how intense the pressure in those situations is and how someone, even with JK's experience and talent, is not immune from it. The slightest tension in any part of the body can result in the ball not going where it is intended and JK's final ball, only a matter of inches from being a perfect yorker on leg-stump, was awry enough for Eddie Hemmings, a man who once made 95 in an Ashes Test, to slice it past point for four.

Ever the team man JK was contrite beyond measure, which was entirely in keeping but unnecessary for someone who had given himself so often and so selflessly to the cause. I don't know whether he had already made his mind up to retire that season, but that moment seemed to seal matters. Two months later he'd called it a day.

It is not too far-fetched to say that he carried Essex's bowling for the decade between 1977 and 1987. The county certainly based much of their strategy around him. In my time at the club, Keith Fletcher used to look at the fixture list and surmise that Essex would probably need 12 or 13 victories to clinch the county championship title and began identifying where and against whom, weather permitting, they might come.

"JK will win us four or five with the ball, Goochie three or four with the bat, the other bowlers and batsmen a couple each," he used to say. It was a reductive approach, and ridiculously facile for such a complex game, but it was uncanny how often Fletch's gnomic prophesies came good.

So valuable was JK, especially when it was swinging, that Fletch once sent the entire team after play (bar JK), to go and look for a ball that Imran Khan had hit over the east wall at Hove. Before it had been lost, JK had been swinging it round corners while its replacement had not moved off the straight. We found it, too, in someone's back garden and next morning normal service was resumed with JK running through Sussex to finish with seven for 55, as Essex prevailed by an innings and 53 runs.

Essex won the county championship four times during JK's career. On three of those occasions, 1979, 1983 and 1984, he took over 100 first-class wickets during the season. Only in 1986 did Essex win the title without him being the club's leading wicket taker, his 58 victims eclipsed by Neil Foster and John Childs.

Essex's fortunes, especially in the longer game, were closely linked to JK's fitness and form. In 1987, with knee injuries limiting his appearances, he took just 26 wickets at 34, his worst haul since becoming established in the side almost two decades earlier. As a result, Essex finished 12th in the table, their lowest position for 13 years.

The public, especially Essex supporters, loved and appreciated him. Alan Davies, the actor who plays Jonathan Creek, and an Essex fan, even chose JK as his schoolboy hero, penning a portrait of him in a book entitled *My Favourite Cricketer*. His was not a lone assessment.

JK's on-field heroics were only part of his allure. Fun-loving, stoic, selfless and a coper by nature, he was the ideal companion in a small hunter-gatherer group like a cricket team. Today's coaches talk about having leaders throughout the team and, while JK never sought any office higher than senior pro, his deeds and words oozed authority and commitment.

Serious when it mattered, he also possessed a levity when the moment allowed, like the time he bowled a gentle full toss first ball after tea, with an orange. Not being forewarned, John Hopkins, the Glamorgan batsman, struck it with relish for what he thought was an easy boundary, his disappointment palpable when four pips slid from his bat rather than four runs.

Another time, when a final batting point looked beyond Essex in a Championship match against Kent, he shouldered arms to a straight one from Graham Dilley and lost his middle stump. It was simple, he said, when I asked him whether he had lost sight of the ball. Although he didn't like Kent, he liked Dill and felt, as part of the old fast bowlers' union, that he deserved another wicket.

A good traveller, he went on five overseas tours with England but played only 21 Tests, foreign conditions perhaps suiting the man more than the bowler. Mind you, it never looked that way after his sensational Test debut against India in Delhi. There, at the ramshackle Ferozeshah Kotla ground, he made a fifty at number nine and took 10 wickets in an England victory.

His seven for 46 in India's first innings came after the umpires changed a misshapen ball that had not swung, something its replacement did to devastating effect. After the game he and Tony Greig, having both attended the post-match press conference, had to flag down two motorcyclists to take them back to their hotel, the rest of the team having already departed in the team bus.

"There were no taxis around so Greigy just waded into the traffic and stopped two blokes on their motorbikes," recalled Lever. "It was an interesting experience to say the least, weaving about during rush hour riding pillion. Of course Greigy loved it and kept urging his driver to go faster."

That tour, which England won 3-1, brought both joy and anguish to JK. That performance in Delhi, plus the other 16 wickets he took, played a large part in England's success. But the elation was soured by accusations of cheating from India's captain, Bishan Bedi, as well as the Indian press. Bedi, who'd been under pressure due to the poor results, claimed that the vaseline gauzes JK and other England bowlers were wearing to keep sweat from their eyes in steamy Madras, were being used to preserve the shine on the ball.

Not many bowlers are paragons of virtue but if JK and his colleagues had wanted to apply vaseline to the ball they would surely not have displayed it so prominently. Unhappily, the controversy has dogged him ever since and he recently considered legal action against an English newspaper which he felt had got its facts wrong when it reprised the affair a couple of years ago.

Although a respecter of authority JK was no 'yes' man, but he was not a rebel either, save for when he decamped to South Africa in 1982 to join other England players for an illicit series against South Africa. A three-year ban on playing for England ensued, with huge benefits to Essex with international duty no longer a distraction.

If he disagreed with his captain's tactics he'd debate the subject, sometimes urgently, but always with respect. His advice, too, especially to lesser mortals, was always considered and never less than helpful. He'd factor in skill levels too so whereas Ian Botham might say to an incoming batsman, "if Lillee drops short just hook him for six," expecting others to do as he would, JK's advice would be more carefully tailored.

When I first joined Essex between school and university, he and Ray East, Essex's mercurial left-arm spinner, took me into their care. Although united by their sense of fun, the pair were not only very different bowlers but different characters too – JK being calm and considered; East volatile and highly strung.

Not every callow teenager fresh from school would have relished guidance from such a colourful duo, but I lapped it up. Once, on an early season away trip to play Leicestershire, the pair took me to a nightclub. The trouble was Essex were playing the next day and I wasn't sure this was the best way to make a good impression.

Imagine my relief, then, when the bouncers told us that we needed jackets to get in. The trouble was, JK had three in the back of his car, including his latest MCC touring blazer which I'm sure he made me wear as some kind of social experiment. As, he gleefully put it at the time, "No self-respecting bird is going to go anywhere near someone wearing a jacket with piping on it, especially when it's two sizes too small." He was not wrong.

Although best mates, nowhere was the difference between my two 'guardians' better exemplified than how they spent their evening meal money at away games, a per diem then of about £6 with the captain getting double so he could buy the occasional round of drinks.

East, who smoked and drank, would use the allowance to buy beer in the bar of the team hotel, usually a Trust House Forte. His 'meal' would comprise several pints and half a packet of cigarettes, which he smoked rather than ate. The only solids he consumed were the complimentary peanuts and stuffed olives Trust House hotels used to provide back then.

Being a good pro, JK was more scientific. As the hardest-working fast bowler in the country – the enormous length of his run-up saw to that – he needed to rehydrate first after a day's play and usually headed to the nearest decent pub to slake his thirst with at least five pints of ale.

When he was satisfied that liquid levels had been replenished, the hunt for the best curry house would commence. Poppadoms, starter and main course were washed down by a few more pints, this time lager, before he hooked up with Easty for a night cap back at the team hotel. The next day JK, his eyes clear and hands steady but sweating a noxious mix of beer fumes and garlic, would be ready for the fray – a man of iron constitution.

In 1986, JK and I played a Test match together, at Headingley, after the selectors picked him for the second Test against India at the grand old age of 37. He took six wickets and I took seven, albeit in a losing cause.

He was his usual calm self except for his insistence that I wake him early on the morning of the match and allow him to travel with me to the ground. When I asked why, he said he'd once missed the start of a Test at Trent Bridge after he'd overslept, a massive faux pas compounded by his getting lost around Nottingham's one-way system.

Although he knew he was to be 12th man on that occasion, the public did not, and he recounted his acute embarrassment when other motorists caught in the traffic began tut-tutting at him and pointing to their watches. In those days most players drove sponsored cars with their names displayed on the bodywork, so arriving incognito was impossible.

Ordinarily, such tardiness would have attracted a big fine from the team enforcer, the physiotherapist Bernard Thomas. But JK escaped censure, his standing as the paragon of team-mates placing him on the same rung as a saint. And saints get martyred, not fined by the physio.

Marlon Hayes, Stephen Chalke and former Somerset cricketer Ken Biddulph

The eleventh men
& Marlon Hayes

by Stephen Chalke

Stephen Chalke played cricket for many years for The Journeymen, the wandering club he co-founded, and for various clubs near his home in Bath. He has written 15 books on cricket, most recently *Summer's Crown – The Story of Cricket's County Championship*.

Marlon Hayes still plays cricket for The Journeymen.

"You don't fancy a game of cricket, do you?"

Throughout my playing days I always seemed to be the one who raised the team – and, to be honest, there was a slightly mad part of me that revelled in the challenge. "On Sunday? … Tomorrow? … This afternoon?" I never gave up. Always, however great the sense of despair, I contrived to sound optimistic. "I'm told you're just the person I'm looking for … We're not often short like this … Don't worry, the latest forecast is for this rain to clear by one o'clock." All lies, of course.

The last-minute drop-outs are the real killers, especially when the weather is iffy. Always the same people, the excuses never quite sounding genuine: "It's not still on this afternoon, is it? ... Only I'll tell you what it is. I've just ricked my back pushing a trolley in Sainsbury's."

You've only just got the team up to eleven. That great moment, with its surge of euphoria. After 29 phone calls. "I'm sorry to let you down," he says cheerfully. "I'm sure you've got plenty of other people you can ask." You look out of the window, and the drizzle has thickened.

It always starts the same way. A sheet of paper, with a batting order, a captain and keeper, and some bowlers. There is a vacancy, and you try to fill it with a decent player. You have a few people in mind – mostly those frustrating characters who have oodles of talent but never seem to have the time. "I'd love to," one of them tells you on Monday. "I've been thinking how much I'd like a game. I'll let you know in a day or two. It all depends whether Jane has to go in to work on Sunday." You add his name in pencil, dreaming of his runs and wickets, but by Thursday you know he is not going to ring back – and you've wasted three days, days in which your next-best bets have all found other things to do: "What a pity you didn't ring yesterday. We've just bought tickets for the air show."

I finished my playing days as captain of a club third eleven. That did test my sanity. My last year in charge was a wet one, dampening the enthusiasm throughout the three elevens, and the second-team captain, knowing he could take my players ("They're not *your* players, they're the club's"), often left it late in the week to get up his Saturday side. 'How many have you got?' he texted one Friday morning. 'I'm down to five, and the firsts want two of them.' We spent the whole evening completing the three elevens, even persuading a couple of crocks out of retirement; then the next day it rained.

The Journeymen were a challenge in a different way. We were a team of friends, with some good players amongst us, but we lived all over the place – from Ipswich to Bristol, from the South Coast to the Peak District – and we met for weekends and mini-tours through the summer. At one stage the fixture list got up to 29 matches, and I played every one of them.

On the whole we were a reliable bunch – though for a while we did have a chap, a social worker, who struggled with the finer details of the fixture card. He had been an opening bowler with Warwickshire Under-19s – twenty years earlier or, as one wag unkindly put it, "eight stone ago". "I'm in the village," he phoned one day just as we were starting our innings at Saham Toney in Norfolk. "Where's the ground?" Three phone calls, copious directions and much confusion later, it turned out he was in Soham, forty miles away in Cambridgeshire.

When we were short, it was always a problem. It was a long day out, far from anywhere. As a wandering side, I tried to put out appropriate teams to give our hosts a good game – but sometimes, finding a last-minute filler went badly wrong. Against a little village side in north Essex, our opening batsman promised to bring along somebody from his Ipswich club side. Unfortunately the only somebody he could find was their professional, a lightning-quick Grenadian fast bowler. We played him as a batsman, he hit a lightning-quick hundred, and our hosts dropped the fixture.

That was not common, though. Far more often, however hard we tried to make him at home and work him into the game, our last-minute recruit proved of little help to the cause.

One chap, rushing around the M25 after 18 holes of golf, pulled up lame the first time he chased a ball in the field. Another was sick early in our innings and spent the afternoon lying on his back in the dressing room, waiting for his lift home. A third, arriving on the ground as we were taking the field, told us he was a fast bowler. He looked the part – tall and rangy – so, with no evidence to the contrary, we gave him the new ball. It was a new fixture, we were trying to make a good impression, and we only got through his over of slow-medium dobbers when the umpire took pity and decided not to call any further wides. He's become something big in the world of television films and 25 years on, whenever I see his name on the closing credits, I smile.

"Do give me a ring if you're ever short," they would say as they left, but mostly we never saw them again.

An exception was our South African opener, Nigel, who made up numbers in a game back in 1990. Full of enthusiasm he brought along his father to umpire and was promptly bowled first ball by a full toss. Yet, undeterred, he did come back, turning himself into a regular who is now our all-time highest run-scorer (and counting). Three years ago, when he was selected for the Essex Over-60s, he told us cheerfully, "At least I can't do any worse than on my Journeymen debut." Perhaps it was an unwise thing to say. The next week he reported back to us that, off the very first delivery of the match, he had been run out without facing a ball.

Sometimes the opposition would find us an eleventh man, but I can't recall any of them coming good. One bloke in Derbyshire was bitter that his own team never selected him: "I'll show them; I'm a far better batsman than most of them." Impressed by his spirit, we put him in at number three, but second ball he had an awful swipe and was caught at mid-wicket. Then, taking pity on him, we gave him a bowl, and that cost us a few runs we could ill afford.

In truth, there were days when we would have been better with ten. There was a 40-over match when we only needed 130-odd to win and were cruising to victory. Our newcomer that day was an architect who had played in the first eleven at Rugby, on which basis we put him in at number five. He lost all track of the match situation and, despite several mid-pitch conferences, hogged the strike for 12 overs in which he scored just seven runs. As a result, despite having several wickets in hand, we got to the last two balls still needing five to win. It was agony to watch but, to our great relief, our big-hitting all-rounder Marlon struck the ball far over the long-on boundary. It allowed our befuddled newcomer to share the glow of victory. In the bar one of the opposition asked him why he had played the whole game in a blue-and-white-striped Guernsey sweater. "Was it that noticeable?" he asked.

Sadder was the story of an accountant called Toby who arrived at the Hertfordshire ground in a camper van with his three young boys. He was a lovely man, and he did play regular village cricket. But it just wasn't his day. My friend John launched our innings with a sparkling cameo which included a six that smashed the back window of Toby's van. Then, when John was dismissed by a running catch in the deep, Toby replaced him at the crease. He played and missed three balls, was bowled 'all ends up' by the fourth and returned to the side of his camper van. As he started to remove his pads, one of his boys – he couldn't have been more than seven years old – delivered his verdict. "You were hopeless, Daddy," he said. "Really awful. I bet they wish they hadn't asked you."

I think my brother Andrew best summed up these players. He was the non-striker in a game when I was the bowler's end umpire and a last-minute recruit, a *Times* journalist, came out to bat. Put in at number six in that nice way we treated our newcomers, he clubbed his first ball over mid-wicket's head for two runs. I turned to Andrew: "Wouldn't it be nice if for once one of these guys hit twenty or thirty?" "Just treat the two as a bonus," he said, and the bloke was bowled next ball.

There were days, though, when our late call-ups surprised us. Some even surprised themselves, none more so than Simon, a furniture restorer who played for us in an all-day fixture at the Cambridge University ground, Fenner's. He was out cheaply before lunch, and we didn't need his wicket-keeping, but late in the day, with the game drifting towards a draw, we indulged his wish to have a rare bowl. He tossed up some invitingly slow leg-breaks, took five quick wickets and won us the match. It was the best day of his cricketing life.

A week later, he rang. "Nobody at my club believes me. You couldn't photocopy the scorebook page, could you?" He had it framed and hung it in his hall; I expect it's still there. His day out with the Journeymen.

When I was living in London in the 1980s, I had a spell of getting up the team for a club that played in the public parks. This introduced another element into the afternoon: the unattached cricketers who would hang around with their kit, hoping to find a side who were one short. One regular, a minicab driver, pitched up one day when both teams had only ten. He spoke to the opposition captain, then came over to us: "He says, if I play for them, I can bat at number three and bowl first change. What are you offering?"

On another occasion Johnny, our Jamaican all-rounder, turned up at the last minute, hoping we would be one short. We weren't so he walked across to the other match in the field. All the players were black, and he returned happy; he'd got himself a game. He picked up his kit bag, and off he went. A few minutes later he was walking back towards us, still carrying his bag. "It's no good," he said. "They're all Jehovah's Witnesses. They're not allowed to play with anybody else."

The Journeymen were always immensely grateful to the last-minute recruits and, in our all too English way, tended to put up with things we would never have tolerated from a regular. Like the primary school headmaster, a young South African, who thought it OK at a beautiful Oxford college ground to come out to field with a fag and a can of lager. Nobody had the heart to tell him we didn't play our cricket like that. Or the investment analyst, a newcomer to cricket, who responded to the question "Who wants to start the umpiring?" by enthusiastically seizing the white coat and sticking his finger up at every half-appeal. We were three down before anybody broke through the politeness barrier and hauled him off. Or the college lecturer who spent ages scoring hardly any runs, then at tea announced that, if it was all right with us, he wouldn't bother to stay for the fielding.

Not that we always finished up with eleven. On the first morning of a five-day Journeymen tour to the West Country, our off-spinner dropped out at a quarter to nine: "The car's playing up, and I've got a bit of a sore throat coming on." I don't know why, but I was always rather suspicious of people who offered two excuses.

Then, with all my efforts to replace him failing (including a forlorn attempt to sign up the assistant in the town's sports shop), another team member of those early days – a rather precious soul – declared our meeting-place pub unsuitable for his new baby, went off in search of somewhere healthier and did not appear at the ground till an hour after the start. Inevitably, with only nine men present, we had to field first.

Marlon took the new ball and, in his third over, he turned to me at mid-off: "I'll slip in a fast yorker." No sooner had he released the ball than he pulled up in agony. The ball flew back over his head, landing with a splash in the stream. He did not bowl again that summer – it turned out he had slipped a disc – but, being Marlon, he insisted on staying on the field. With our threadbare ten men, we were 18 for six, chasing 257, when he went in to bat, and we finished on 184 for six for an honourable draw. In agony, but not wanting to let the team down, he played all five days on the tour.

Marlon had been sent to England from cricket-mad Barbados at the age of fourteen, in 1970, and he hardly played in his early years in London. Perhaps, in other circumstances, he might have been a leading light in a top Middlesex club, as his half-brother Michael was, but that never seemed to be what he wanted from his cricket. I first came across him in the early 1980s, turning out for a delightfully laid-back park team called the Whitechapel Wonders, a group of ex-students of the London College of Furniture.

Not that I would call Marlon a laid-back cricketer. He gives his all, fielding with an energy that is almost electric, and he wants to win – but only up to a point. Childhood experiences have left him with a deep, if quietly spoken, sense of right and wrong, and he, more than any of us, hates the matches where ill-feeling and unnecessary aggression creep in.

If the truth be known, he holds onto these peace-loving principles more steadfastly than I do. In one game in Surrey, when we needed one last wicket for victory – over a team we did not often beat – a twelve-year-old boy came out to bat. Marlon was bowling downhill, generating real pace, and for several overs the older batsman kept the boy off strike. I bowled the penultimate over, and with a carefully set field I made sure that for the final over the lad would have to face the full force of Marlon. And what happened? Marlon came off two paces and sent down six gentle off-breaks.

"Well batted," he told the youngster as we came off. Then he turned to me with a smile: "In five years' time he'll be hitting us everywhere."

Marlon joined the Journeymen at the start and, like all the best club men, his loyalty has been unwavering, his dedication to the club absolute. In our best years we were a tight-knit group, with several of us playing almost all the matches, but nobody has missed fewer games over the years than Marlon – and he is still going strong. Like me, if we were searching for an eleventh man, he would never give up, never want us to turn up with ten. On one occasion, he told me, when he was working in desperation through an ancient address book, he rang a number, only for a woman to respond in shocked disbelief: "Rahman? Rahman Patel? He died five years ago."

Another time, when someone dropped out the night before a Sunday game ("I've been given a ticket for Captain Beefheart"), I persuaded him to come away from a day with his in-laws. This meant that he had to get up early, take his family from East London down to Tunbridge Wells, then drive the 120 miles to Minster Lovell in Oxfordshire. And back again in the evening, getting home after midnight. The home team were not strong, and the way the game panned out we finished up winning by ten wickets without Marlon having to bat or bowl. In his shoes I would have said something, even if half in jest, but he never grumbled. The team always came first.

At this level of cricket there are factors in team selection about which the professional game knows nothing. At one club with a lot of youngsters, we were forever trying to work out if we had enough cars for the away games. At another club I was told firmly, "You can't leave out Matt; his mother made the tea last week." Then there was the village where somebody had to drop out if at the last minute the owner of the ground fancied a game.

With the Journeymen it was all about fostering a happy team spirit, avoiding the prima donnas and the types who introduce bad feeling into a game. We were lucky in that our best players were all good team men, none more so than Marlon. We had others who scored more runs and took more wickets, though not as all-rounders and not in quite as expressive a way, but there was something about his whole-heartedness, his boundless energy, his generosity, that rubbed off on all of us who played with him – and those who played against him, too, though they didn't always call him by his right name. Martin, Marvin, Mervyn, even Merlin, he's had them all.

For me, that's what being a good team-mate is all about: turning up when you say you will, going that extra mile to help out the team when it's struggling, giving your all to the afternoon and making sure that everybody is made welcome and gets a good game – not least all those last-minute eleventh men. They did add to the fun.

Rodney Marsh

Rodney Marsh

by John Inverarity

John Inverarity played cricket for Western Australia (1962-79), South Australia (1979-85) and Australia (6 Tests, 1968-72). A schoolteacher, he was headmaster of Perth's Hale School (1989-2003). From 2011 to 2014 he was Australia's Chairman of Selectors.

Rodney Marsh played cricket for Western Australia (1968-84) and Australia (96 Tests, 1970-84). He was Director of the Australian Cricket Academy from 1990 to 2001. In 2014 he succeeded John Inverarity as Australia's Chairman of Selectors.

"Hey, man, which billiard table did you borrow those legs from?"

That was Peter Pollock's comment as he looked in amazement at the calves of Rod Marsh whilst the teams enjoyed a post-match dressing-room beer after an Australia v Rest of The World XI unofficial Test match in 1971. Those 'keg-legs', which drew many a comment, served their owner especially well during 96 Tests as one of Australia's finest ever keeper-batsmen. They were the power source for many spectacular dives that resulted in breath-taking catches.

RN (Neil) Harvey, stumped Marsh bowled Mann, 12.

This is how the scorecard from the WACA in 1961/62 read. How could that possibly be? Rodney William Marsh was born in November 1947 and Neil Harvey retired from Test and first-class cricket in March 1963. The gifted left-handed Harvey had skipped down the wicket to one of Tony Mann's well-flighted leg-spinners and driven it beautifully through the covers. The next delivery was similarly well-flighted but it was a googly. One of Australia's greatest players of spin did not pick the googly and was stranded down the wicket. A gleeful 14-year-old keeper removed the bails and, if I remember correctly, a couple of stumps as well.

New South Wales had defeated Western Australia at the WACA in a Sheffield Shield match the day before. Australia's captain and vice-captain, Richie Benaud and Neil Harvey, had agreed to stay on in Perth and guest for the Governor's XI against a Combined Schools XI on the fifth-day pitch on the centre wicket at the WACA. What a thrill for Rod at 14, Tony Mann at 16, yours truly at 17 and the others in the team. That was the first time I had met and played in the same team as Rod Marsh. Even then he was a brilliant keeper and not short of confidence.

The next time I played in a game with Rod, against him this time, was when the University of Western Australia played West Perth in a club semi-final at the WACA in March 1964. Rod was denied the keeping gloves for West Perth by Gordon Becker who was the incumbent keeper-batsman in the Western Australian Shield side. Rod, at 16, top-scored for West Perth with about 70 and fielded well in the gully in a closely fought game in which the University prevailed.

Rod was a talented young man. He was strong academically and a very good pianist, his musical ability coming from his father, Ken, who did many gigs as a jazz musician. Rod's older brother Graham had a very successful career as a professional golfer, and Rod himself was a keen and very good young golfer and Australian Rules footballer, to add to his cricketing skills of keeping, batting and bowling as well.

Frustrated that he was unable to keep wickets for West Perth as Becker blocked his way, he changed clubs. He decided that he wanted to play with the University Cricket Club because Tony Mann was getting stacks of wickets for University. Having gained good results in graduating from high school he easily won a university place. But I suspect the University Club and Tony Mann's hard-spun leg-spinners and googlies were a greater pull than was the prospect of academic endeavour.

Rod Marsh began at the University of Western Australia in February 1965, and his first season was the summer of 1965/66. So began the great joy of my playing in the same team with Rod Marsh.

I suspect that Rod was born with a mischievous grin on his face. This grin was in a well-formed mature state by 1965, and university life was an ideal arena for mischief.

When the stocky Rod Marsh made his Test debut in November 1970, he was quite trim relative to how he had been in 1965/66. I fielded at first slip that summer and invariably moved a little wider when his trousers split down the back seam. Each week his mum would sew the seam together again, but her efforts seldom survived the first half-hour of her son's keeping. A number of safety pins were used, but they were no match.

During that first season the University made a big score on the first Saturday, declared and had the Fremantle team one down at stumps. Early in the afternoon the next Saturday Tony Mann settled in for a long spell, bowling his wrist-spinners into the perfect breeze, known as the Fremantle Doctor. A promising young left-hand batsman by the name of Andrews was playing Tony Mann quietly and competently. I was fielding at slip. Rod began to express his displeasure about Tony's bowling. He then began confiding to Andrews, "This guy can't bowl. Why don't you use your feet? Get down the wicket and knock him off his length." During the next over he skipped down the wicket, made a half-volley out of Tony's normal leggie and cracked it through the covers. "Great shot," said the keeper.

You've guessed it. The next ball was a perfectly pitched googly and Andrews was stumped by a couple of yards to the great amusement of the keeper and the slip fieldsman. Well, Neil Harvey had made a similar error four years earlier.

At the tea break a bemused Master Andrews looked appealingly at Rod with, "But you suggested I get down the pitch and then you stumped me" written all over his face. Rod put his hand on his shoulder and said, "Good on you. You had exactly the right idea. You just need to get further down the pitch." Master Andrews was reassured. We managed to bowl Fremantle out soon after tea and asked them to follow on. Andrews came in at four. Mann was bowling. Marsh was grinning, mischievously. The keeper offered the batsman further friendly encouragement and advice. The batsman took it and skipped down the wicket, even further, and smacked the bowler through the covers. "Great shot" was heard from behind the stumps. Three balls later was the beautifully flighted googly. Same result. Andrews, stumped Marsh bowled Mann. Twice on the same afternoon.

Rod's academic progress was no match for his development as a cricketer. He was selected to play for Western Australia against the touring West Indians early in the summer of 1968/69 as he was about to turn 21. It was a four-day fixture during the university examination period.

In 2008 I was invited to a Balliol College reunion in Nedlands, a suburb of Perth. At that function I was chatting to an elderly Professor of Geography at the University of Western Australia. After a time he said, "I presume you know Rod Marsh. Do you keep in touch with him?" I answered in the affirmative. "Well, I still have his Geography 200 examination script from 1968 in my office." I enquired further and we then enjoyed a good chuckle together. I asked the professor if he would post to me a copy of what Rod had submitted. Three days later it arrived. It read: "Dear Professor, I have a pressing engagement at the WACA and I am unable to stay any longer. I request a deferment and hope to sit the paper in January, cricket commitments permitting. Yours sincerely, Rod Marsh." I was delighted to receive that piece of paper and immediately called Rod. He recalled it all clearly, but added, "I had no intention of ruining my summer and sitting the paper in January."

That professor was not the same professor who summoned Rod to his study towards the end of Rod's first year at university. Whilst admonishing the student for not handing in a couple of assignments, the professor said, "Well then, young man, why have you chosen to come to university?" "To play cricket," came the firm response. There was a bit of a chuckle then, "No, seriously, why have you come to university? What do you aspire to whilst you are here?" "I've just told you. I've come here because of the cricket. I aspire to get into the State team and then the Australian team." The firm and grumpy response was, "Son, you'll never make a living out of cricket." Fifteen years later Rod and his family moved into a lovely home just a few doors from the professor who had admonished him.

After play, whilst we were at university, we would all go out together and have a lot of fun. We would sometimes scheme up unusual ways in which we could dismiss the opposition. Amidst a great deal of laughter a detailed and improbable plan was hatched. It was put into action during a three-day inter-varsity game in which Rod Marsh was captain and Tony Mann his lively lieutenant. The University was cruising to an easy victory when an earnest and tentative number eleven, who did not bowl, came to the wicket and was at the non-striker's end.

The plan was this. The medium-fast bowler would send one down the leg-side. Keeper Marsh would take the ball, but curse as if he had missed it. First slip and leg slip would turn and 'chase', heading for the sightscreen. Fine leg would race around the boundary towards the sight screen in an attempt to cut off the seemingly missed delivery. The plan was executed perfectly. Rod ambled up to the stumps, ball hidden within gloved hand. The puzzled non-striker could not see the ball going towards the boundary but was persuaded by the frenzy of activity heading towards the sightscreen. The hesitant non-striker eventually called the other batsman through.

When the number eleven was within about five yards of his crease Rod showed him the ball and, with that renowned mischievous grin, removed the bails. The umpire honoured the appeal. After a few moments of hilarity the batsman was recalled and restored. The team generously made sure that the number eleven made some runs before the game was completed with the fall of that final wicket. The carefully planned run-out received a prolonged airing at the post-match celebrations the teams shared together.

Rod Marsh was an outstanding cricketer, tough competitor and warm-hearted and amusing team-mate. He was, also, one of the fairest and most sportsmanlike cricketers I ever played with. His disclaiming of a catch towards the end of the gripping Centenary Test at the MCG in 1977 when the umpire and his team-mates thought he had made a clean catch was one of many such examples of his fairness and integrity.

This reminds me of a story about Rod when he was touring India with an England Lions team in about 2004 or 2005. The India A wicket-keeper came to Rod, wobbled his head and said, "Please, Mr Marsh, sir, would you please watch my keeping and at the end of the game provide me with a couple of tips from what you have seen?" "OK," was the reply. Three days later the Indian lad duly enquired of his idol. Rod apologised that, as he had been concentrating on his own players, he had not noticed his keeping, but promised to watch him closely during the next game. At the conclusion of the next game the Indian keeper hurried up to Rod and said, "Please, Mr Marsh, could you please give me a tip now."

Rod's firm and emphatic response was, "Yes, young man. Stop cheating!"

"Oh, yes. Certainly. Thank you very much, sir."

John Spencer

John Spencer

by John Barclay

John Barclay played cricket for Sussex (1970-86). In 1986 he was appointed director of the newly formed Arundel Castle Cricket Foundation, a position which he still holds.

John Spencer played cricket for Cambridge University (1970-72) and Sussex (1969-80). A teacher of geography, he was Deputy Head of Brighton College till his retirement in 2012.

He was not a natural athlete. Tallish he was for sure and with an untidy mop of fair hair, and built more for stamina and long distance than the sprint. More of a Red Rum than a Shergar. For all that, he was the fastest bowler I had ever faced, by a long way, when we first met up in a match between Brighton and Horsham in 1967 at the Withdean stadium, more recently well known for hosting Brighton and Hove Albion's home matches whilst they awaited the completion of their new ground on the South Downs.

I, aged thirteen, was opening the batting for Horsham with a largish man, somewhat my senior, Doughy Baker. I was the youngest participant by some distance, easily identified from my smooth features and squeaky voice. I may just have graduated to wearing a box – a pink one and reputedly brittle. Despite these mountains of insecurity to be overcome, I took guard and became aware of the mighty Spencer, well known already to all but me, pounding in to bowl. Thrusting forward my front leg I was greeted by the reassuring clunk of ball upon bat. I had hit one, and although neither my partnership with Doughy nor my encounter with Spencer lasted long, it was the beginning of a friendship, understanding and respect that has lasted for some fifty years.

Spencer, I discovered, was different from most bowlers. For a start he was highly intelligent with an inquiring mind, good with people and funny too. In an era when Oxford and Cambridge Universities still absorbed talented sportsmen, bowlers were distinctly uncommon – indeed, at the time, few wanted to try their hand on the gentle batting surfaces of Fenner's and the Parks. But Cambridge had a profound effect upon Spencer. Under the direction and captaincy of Majid Khan who became one of his firm friends for life, his cricket and subsequent confidence blossomed. A degree in geography would later become the pillar for his teaching career but, most important of all, there he met his future wife, Catherine, with whom he has fashioned the closest partnership of all.

By the time I played against John at Cambridge, and even though I didn't actually face his bowling there, my brief innings being brought to its conclusion up the other end, I had begun to get to know him better through hours of practice in the nets at Hove. He was determined to master the skills of swing and seam and at the same time to strengthen himself for the task. In those days there was little scientific about training programmes. So he would bowl and I would bat. That was the arrangement. In the freezing cold we would practise, spurred on by the prospect of lunch, warmth and temporary respite provided by the Sussex Cricketer Hotel at the gates to the ground. Little thought, if any, was then given to the diet of professional cricketers or their health in general – most smoked heavily and we filled ourselves up liberally with whatever was going. Spencer, if I remember rightly, was particularly fond of potatoes, which he piled up high on his plate each day. These fuelled his energy and stamina, at least that's what he'd say. As a result he acquired the nickname 'Spud', with which he was saddled for the rest of his career. So, from my point of view, it was a case of "Spud, would you mind bowling to me?" This I would ask frequently because he loved bowling and knew I was a willing target and keen to learn. Rarely did he turn me down. What he liked to do was to bowl eight consecutive overs in the nets at one batsman without interruption from any other bowlers. It was an exercise of strict discipline and concentration. We rarely spoke. I would simply bat as best I could and throw the ball back to him – always the same ball which was vigorously shined and carefully tended. I was in fact the ideal batsman, rarely offering a powerful or aggressive shot and so allowing John to establish and maintain his precious rhythm throughout. Thus we became friends, based upon mutual respect combined with a deep and ambitious desire to excel.

It was in those early days that John, more than anyone else, showed me the way and helped me to belong. A team, I have found, tends not to work so well until its component parts are valued. I was only sixteen when first selected to play for Sussex and so something of an outsider. Nobody quite knew why I was playing and neither did I. We were destined for Swansea to play Glamorgan who, at that time in August 1970, were sitting at the top of the table. Lewis (captain), Majid Khan, Shepherd, Davis (more than one), Nash, Cordle, Jones (more than one), Walker and others – legendary Welsh (mostly) names.

John was my friend on this trip and just about the only player I really knew. He showed me where to change and generally steered me in the right direction. My tasks were varied. Not only did I have to play cricket but I also had to double up as twelfth man as only eleven Sussex players had travelled to Swansea, presumably to save on expenses. All sorts of duties had to be undertaken – collect the valuables, make a drinks list for the players and take orders for lunches to be consumed in the dressing room. All this was new to me and came as something of a surprise. The cricket seemed to be of secondary importance. Spencer kept me on track.

For three days we muddled through, spared any major embarrassments by the weather. For most of the time it rained. Grey skies prevailed, mostly light drizzle, the sea disappearing and then reappearing again for a moment as a kindly gesture. I did get to bat eventually. Like many before me I spent longer walking down and then up all the pavilion steps at the St Helen's ground than I did batting – out second ball, lbw Nash for 0, disconcerted as much as anything else by the Jones brothers chatting to each other in Welsh. "What were they saying?" I wondered. Whatever it was it did it for me.

"Many have made nought on their debut," John reminded me as I sat in a corner of the dressing room somewhat crestfallen. "In fact I think the same might have happened to me." Some attempt at comfort. That was it for batting. We spent the rest of the match fielding. The pitch, uncovered of course, had become severely affected by the weather. In racing parlance it might have been described as soft, heavy in places. Encouraged by this Jim Parks, the Sussex captain, declared our second innings prematurely after just three overs batting, setting Glamorgan, in a distant era which can now scarcely be imagined and when things were done differently, a target of 154 runs to win in 90 minutes as well as the compulsory 20 overs in the last hour. There was just a chance I might get a bowl and maybe exploit these treacherous conditions. It was considered to be a sporting declaration which, loosely translated, usually means the captain has got it wrong.

In the event Glamorgan reached the target with much time to spare. My bowling was not required partly because gentle off-spin was clearly not the answer in the conditions, but also I had slightly pulled a thigh muscle attempting to take a catch running back from mid-on. When it was all over I limped apologetically from the field downcast along with the rest of the team. "Don't forget the drinks,'" Spencer reminded me as I hobbled up the steps. The drinks were those I had ordered earlier in the day and would now be waiting, hopefully, for me to collect on the bar – pints of milk and beer mainly and a whisky for the scorer who had a dicky bladder. "Do you want a hand?" John said. "No, I'll be all right."

Off I went to the bar where crowds of happy Welshmen were celebrating Glamorgan's victory and position at the top of the championship table. There was a fair amount of jostling and shoving but eventually I got a grip on the tray, balanced myself and began my stuttering journey back down the stairs to the dressing room. Though I say it myself, I made reasonable progress and tentatively pushed open the door to be greeted by a smell of damp clothing and wet towels, at which point I stumbled, only slightly, but just enough to throw me out of kilter for a moment and send the drinks sliding down the tray with irreversible momentum. "Look out," someone shouted but, as is usually the case when such warnings are made, it was too late. One by one rather than altogether the glasses and their contents were pitched into Tony Greig's cricket case. Quelled by the shock of this dilemma nobody spoke for a few seconds – it seemed like an age – while we all observed Greig's batting gloves and box, which incidentally made quite a good boat and had yet to capsize, floating in a rich cocktail of milk and beer, mildly flavoured by the whisky as well as the other unsavoury contents of the cricket case.

As I observed the scene before me, I could tell my belonging to the team had rather gone out of the window, what with making no contribution in the match, and now this mortifying calamity seemed likely to scar me for life. It was too awful and, looking back, the worst moment of my professional career. And into Greig's case of all places – yet perhaps it did have something of a bonding effect. Spencer remained on my side and a supporter whilst, ironically, in the subsequent years, Greig would have a profound effect upon the development of John's career and indeed mine.

By 1973 Spencer had joined the team full-time after a successful three years at Cambridge. His presence came as a breath of fresh air for everyone and coincided with Greig's first year as captain. Greig and Spencer went about things in the same way; both blond, tall and enthusiastic, they exuded energy and, unlike many professional cricketers, were actually keen to play. Not for them lounging about playing cards and staring balefully out of the window praying for rain. Strangely, you might think, bad weather heralded much joy in the dressing room.

So it was good to have Spencer back in the side for the first match of the season played in early May against Kent at Hastings – midweek, not really a show-stopper with which to kick the season off. But there it was – for three days we trundled off to Hastings and back through the rush-hour traffic to play against our rivals and neighbours. I was happy enough to be selected.

Kent batted first on a cold and cloudy morning. Few people, so far as I can remember, were watching, but I was given a bowl before lunch and trundled away with my off-breaks. It was a bygone age when spinners were treated with some respect and not destroyed out of hand. Greig, fielding at mid-wicket, clapped his hands a lot. And then I took a wicket. Graham Johnson played over a full-length ball and was bowled, deceived by the flight maybe. I like to think so. Lunch presented an opportunity to warm up the hands and enjoy that tingling sensation of blood coursing back into the fingers.

The gulls, so vociferous in the morning, seemed more subdued after lunch as if contemplating their next course of action whilst Cowdrey and Denness batted elegantly and with effortless ease. But cricket is nothing if not surprising. In mid-afternoon, while the real world was busy getting on with its life, Cowdrey, possibly lulled into some sort of trance by the hypnotic atmosphere, clipped one of my gentle half-volleys at catchable height straight to Greig fielding at mid-wicket. How can a game that consistently brings about such misery and upset even, if for a brief moment, afford such heartfelt joy? It was, of course, run-of-the-mill stuff for the rest of the team and I don't think it lifted the spirits of the gulls that much, but I was transformed and uplifted by the sheer delight of claiming the wicket of a great player. Spencer would have come over to me too and perhaps said something like, "Well, there you are, it's not as difficult as all that, is it?" I felt the warmth of playing my part and being accepted.

That was the end of the first day. Kent had made a useful score to be getting on with, just short of 300. Now it was our turn. That night back at home in Brighton I was woken in the early hours by thunder and the next day travelled, through puddles and minor flooding, back to Hastings. Now, you will bear in mind that in those days the pitches were left uncovered from as soon as a match began and open to the elements.

"Doubt if we'll play today. Probably flooded." That was the general verdict from my passengers and I got the distinct feeling that a day in the pavilion might be preferable to facing Underwood on a wet pitch. His reputation in such circumstances was formidable and his ruthless exploitation of the slightest dampness legendary. I remember we sat about for hours in scattered groups fervently hoping we would not have to play. Some of us went shopping in Hastings, one or two even visited the Old Harbour and seaside. I chose to hang about around the pavilion where Spencer gave me some much-needed coaching – how to face Underwood on a wet pitch – not yet in the manual. Despite my poor past form, a highest score so far of 25, I had been promoted to number seven in the order. Spencer bowled some tricky balls across the dressing room which, on the uneven surface, had to be treated with respect. Then I bowled to him. The windows were in some danger, of course, but the indoor games passed the time till lunch and for most of the afternoon until an early tea was taken. This was a worry as it implied the umpires, Bill Alley and Ken Palmer – a distinguished pair of Somerset players in their day and so well used to the vagaries of the weather – might be considering a start, which indeed they were.

I went out to bat with the evening shadows from a watery sun stretching out over the ground. At 57 for five I took guard to face Underwood with fielders clustered all around – Woolmer at point, Ealham and Luckhurst short-legs, Johnson and Cowdrey in the slips, Asif at gully, Knott keeping wicket. All were to become friends in due course but for now it was the silence that caused such fear. Underwood ran in to bowl and emerged at the last moment from behind the umpire before snapping into his vigorous action. The ball, not a slow one, whirred as it approached, I pushed out my front leg with bat accompanying alongside as Spencer had assiduously taught me. But the ball collided with neither. Instead it spat at me spitefully removing a small piece of soil from the pitch and struck me a painful blow on my right thumb whence it looped benignly to Cowdrey at slip. Out first ball. Spencer followed shortly afterwards and, back in the pavilion, uttered the consoling words, "As long as you live, you'll never learn to play a ball like that – even with my coaching."

Further storms and heavy rain loomed in from the west and seemed to target Hastings. On arrival at the ground for the final day, what we saw gave us hope that surely this time there would be no chance of play. There was more water than grass to be seen. Apparently the high tide – according to Spencer, the geographer – left a basin of moisture with nowhere to go. There was no question of practice or warm-up, just a matter of allowing time to slip by as we awaited our fate.

The tide began to ebb as tides do and nature took its course – but what was not natural was the surprise presence of the local fire brigade who descended upon the ground with sirens blaring and proceeded to pump gallons of water off the saturated outfield. I'm not sure about the sirens – I might have made them up – but I well remember the Kent players with trousers rolled up to the knees sweeping away as much water as they could whilst the Sussex team stood idly by. Fortunately there was no crowd to speak of, otherwise they might have joined in too.

The upshot of all these shenanigans was that conditions were deemed fit for play by four o'clock after another early tea. This time my practice in the pavilion took place as we began our second innings. Spencer and indeed the rest of the team did not hold back from reminding me that I was 'on a king pair': two first-ball dismissals in the same match. At 22 for five I walked timidly out to bat again. The scene was somewhat similar to that of the day before. The sun was shining, the tide was out and Underwood was bowling. His first ball, his quicker one, was really quite fast. I pushed out and the ball struck my bat firmly – good to hit one – only to witness Luckhurst at short leg thrust out his left hand and so prevent my scoring. I had at least averted the king pair. The next ball was slower and more devilishly spun. With the forward defensive shot embedded in my brain, I eased forward only to experience the same painful sensation upon my right thumb whence, once again, the ball travelled without fuss to Cowdrey at slip. I returned in a lowly state to the pavilion where I was greeted on the steps by Spencer wreathed in smiles. "Bad luck," he said, with endearing warmth, "but nothing was ever more certain than that you were going to get a pair. It will never get this bad again." And indeed it never did.

It didn't take me long to realise that John was a great teacher in the making. His enthusiasm and energy rubbed off on the young who were inspired by his expertise, speed of thought and mild eccentricity. He had all the ingredients with which to enhance the world of education. His mentor, Greig, had some of the same traits but was more overtly ambitious and quickly became aware of his own commercial potential. Whilst Greig was more interested in money and what it offered, Spencer was more grounded – the family and home life meant everything to him. His bonfire and vegetables were the backbone to his sporting and teaching career. He found his niche and revelled in it. As the years went by he became something of a legend amongst the pupils he taught at Brighton College.

It was Greig who gave him a leg-up in 1977 when he invited John to head a major coaching initiative based at Cranbrook School in Sydney. This programme was to run alongside the early stages of World Series Cricket, a scheme which, at the time, threatened to tear apart the established world of cricket. Kerry Packer, the head of a vast media empire, was the man behind it and Greig was hired as his chief recruiting officer and charismatic leader. Youngsters from the length and breadth of the eastern fringes of Australia signed up for the courses by way of Packer's immensely popular and widely circulated *Woman's Weekly* magazine. For six weeks in the summer holidays children converged upon Sydney for cricket coaching that pleased parents as much as their offspring – something to do during the long summer holiday. Spencer was the man in charge and invited me amongst others to join his team of coaches.

For the entire course, and an extra week of private coaching after all was done, I worked with John. Despite the heat and mixed ability of the young I was never bored, never jaded. It was great fun and I was well paid – important for someone saving up to buy a house. Each session would conclude with some sort of match between 'The Spuds' (Spencer's team) and 'The Trouts' (my team). Quite absurd games they were which invariably and mysteriously ended in a tie. Children are easily fooled at that age, a bit of the Father Christmas syndrome. Packer and Greig came to watch from time to time and other stars too – Ian Chappell, Rod Marsh and Ross Edwards. They all joined in. Parents loved it and I remember one mother being particularly grateful. "I drop my boy off at nine," she said, "and he can play cricket till five – not only that, it takes him 2½ hours to get home on the bus. Perfect."

Those courses and working with Spencer taught me a lot, not so much about cricket but more about people. It seemed to me that to be successful consistently the participants must for the most part enjoy themselves. They should be having fun. Greig understood that and began to change the atmosphere of the game in the early seventies. Without doubt Spencer was influenced by this shift away from the habitual dourness that tended to hang over professional cricket. Not that Greig and Spencer were not dedicated, they were, but they also radiated a spark from which I learnt a lot and which I was later given the chance to put into practice when I became captain of Sussex myself in the early eighties.

Make no mistake, behind that enduring facade of mild eccentricity and occasional lunacy, Spencer was a very good bowler and loyal friend and supporter. He might have made a very good captain, too, had the chance come his way.

Adrian Dale

Adrian Dale

by Steve James

Steve James played cricket for Cambridge University (1989-90), Glamorgan (1985-2003) and England (1998, 2 Tests). He also played rugby for Lydney. He has written three books on cricket and writes on both cricket and rugby for the *Daily* and *Sunday Telegraph*.

Adrian Dale played cricket for Glamorgan (1989-2004). He is now the Community Cricket Manager for Auckland Cricket in New Zealand.

Ah, cricketers' nicknames, they can be so banal and so annoying. Not that you ever want to admit the latter, of course. At Glamorgan I acquired the moniker 'Sid', after the 'Carry On' actor. I did not particularly like it, but I never let on. You just hope it will wear off. Sadly that one did not.

From his first days Adrian Dale was known mainly as 'Arthur' after the fictional second-hand car salesman. He never complained about it, and he is still known by that name today. He was also known briefly as 'Floods' because he once came out to field in a new pair of whites that his wife had taken up rather too eagerly. They were so short that it really did look as if he was expecting a flood. That nickname did wear off, but there was another one that was used occasionally by team-mate Robert Croft, though it did not take off. The off-spinning all-rounder sometimes used to call Dale 'Nuts and Bolts'. For once it was a name that concerned the cricket we were supposed to be playing, and it summed Dale up superbly.

Dale was indeed the nuts and bolts of the Glamorgan side of the 1990s and early millennium, the most successful period in the club's history, when a county championship pennant was joyously claimed in 1997 and one-day titles were won in 1993, 2002 and 2004. Dale played a part in all those titles. Indeed he hit the winning runs in 2004 when the Pro40 title was secured at Colwyn Bay against Lancashire. But he was not a leading light.

He was always more Sancho Panza than Don Quixote, leaving the more prominent roles to Matthew Maynard, Hugh Morris, Steve Watkin, Croft, Waqar Younis, Sir Vivian Richards even, Matthew Elliott and Michael Kasprowicz as well. Sometimes even I would do reasonably well.

There was a time when I thought Dale should have done more. In fact, I wrote as much in my autobiography, observing that he had underachieved. Looking back, it was a harsh, even churlish reflection.

Dale was a damn fine county cricketer. He scored over 12,500 first-class runs at an average of 33, with 23 centuries, and took over 200 first-class wickets with his medium-pacers. He also scored over 6,500 runs in one-day cricket, whilst taking over 250 wickets.

Maybe that cold judgement of mine was prompted by his once promising to be something more than he eventually became. For he had been selected to go on an England A tour to South Africa in 1993. It was a strong squad and it did very well, but of the 14 selected only Dale did not go on to play for England in Tests or one-day internationals. I took it as evidence of his underachievement, but maybe he was actually overachieving at the time. He has since admitted to me how difficult he found the game. That was not especially obvious at the time.

Dale had been selected for that trip because of a superb season for Glamorgan in which he had scored a double century against Middlesex, sharing in a partnership of 425 with the great Richards. It is still the highest partnership for any wicket for the county. I have to say that feat of Dale's inspired me. I had not scored a double century at that stage of my career, and, to be frank, had not thought it remotely possible. Dale went and I followed, though I did not score one till a couple of years later.

Dale also helped me more consciously in the advancement of my career. I was going through a particularly lean patch and, aware of my struggles, he pulled me aside at nets one day and asked me a simple question: "Are you watching the ball?"

"Of course I am," I replied.

"No, are you really watching the ball, rather than constantly worrying about your technique?" he said.

I wasn't watching the ball. I knew I wasn't. I was looking in the general direction of the bowler but was not focusing intently on the small red missile in his hand. I vowed immediately to do just that, and it changed my game.

It meant I was not fretting about my backlift or whatever else was my weekly worry at the time. Instead, I was clearing my mind, and when playing my strokes I was leading more with my head down the pitch. One small comment from a team-mate was all it took, but you would be surprised how infrequently it happens. Most cricketers are incredibly self-absorbed.

Glamorgan would kill for a home-grown cricketer like Dale these days. And he was home-grown, despite being born in Germiston, outside Johannesburg. It used to irk him when he was referred to as 'South Africa-born', because his parents were only there for a short time.

His father, John, was a stalwart of Chepstow Cricket Club and Dale grew up at the club. It was only a few miles down the road from Lydney, where I spent most of my summer time at the local club. The England/Wales border might have been between us – Lydney being on the English side, of course – but the two clubs played in the same competition, the now defunct Three Counties League. So Dale and I began as rivals, and to my eternal embarrassment he did once 'bounce' me out in one of those Lydney versus Chepstow matches. But we very soon became friends and team-mates. To say that we travelled the same road would be rather an understatement.

We did indeed travel everywhere together, beginning when we played in the same Glamorgan Colts side in the South Wales League, along with Croft, Watkin and Tony Cottey. All of us were part of the 1997 championship success, yet it was deemed a bad idea to continue with the Colts team.

Our careers were intertwined in so many ways. Rather spookily, to the exact day, we share the record for the youngest centurion in the Three Counties League. I was 16 years and 297 days old when I scored a century against Cirencester in 1984, and Dale was precisely the same age when he passed three figures against Corsham in 1985.

We both attended Swansea University, where in 1988 we were proud to be part of the team that won the UAU competition, defeating in the final a strong Durham side that included Nasser Hussain. We played, along with Hussain, Mike Atherton and others, for the successful Combined Universities team that shocked a number of counties in the 1989 Benson & Hedges Cup.

We spent a winter together in Zimbabwe playing for a black side called Bionics in Harare, a stint I repeated while Dale ventured to New Zealand, where he met his future wife, Ruth, and where he resides now with his three children, Jessica, Luke and Georgina.

We shared flats in Cardiff, shared hotel rooms on away trips and shared bat sponsors. We ended up buying houses next to each other. We basically did everything together, including running so vigorously and successfully between the wickets that it was as if we had some preternatural instincts. We were best mates. Indeed Dale asked me to be best man at his wedding, even if, unfortunately, I could not attend. To play professional cricket with someone like that for around 14 years is special, and surprisingly unusual.

It was not always happiness and harmony. When captain of Glamorgan, I upset Dale hugely by taking the vice-captaincy away from him because it was felt that we were too close and too similar in our views. I handled it clumsily and weakly, informing him by email while he was away in New Zealand and our friendship was never quite the same again. Even then we still had a much stronger friendship than most other players.

There is a lot of talk about the bonds and friendships created by professional sport. In my experience, more often than not, they are exaggerated. Steve Archibald's contention that team spirit is only an illusion glimpsed in the aftermath of victory has become a cliché, but only because it is so very true, especially in cricket, where the long periods when you are thrown together can be detrimental rather than beneficial in such matters.

For you are thrown together, players from different backgrounds and different cultures, with different principles and views. You might be playing a team sport, but cricket is really an individual sport played within the framework of a team environment. Selfishness is everywhere.

Believe me, just to be civil to some of your team-mates can be a trial at times. Respect is the word that is regularly bandied about as the panacea in such situations, and it is true that it is easier to renew a bond with someone who has just won the match for your team. The point is that a cricket dressing room is not always the nest of back-slapping amity it is assumed to be.

For that reason characters like Dale are vital. So often they become rallying points without knowing they are any such thing. They are uncomplaining. They have equanimity. They are not needy. They are not boisterous. They just turn up every day and do their job.

They will always help out that little bit more at net practice and want to do a little more themselves – although Dale once enraged Richards when he arranged to bowl at an Essex batsman before play in a championship match when no Glamorgan batsman wanted a net!

They do not necessarily offer their opinions unless asked but, when they do, it is always worth listening to because it is carefully considered and not just mouthed off in order to sound important.

They are the type who will always back the captain, even when there might be some unrest amongst the troops about him or his decisions. They are the type who will be in charge of the team kitty, trying to keep everyone happy, trying to ensure that everyone gets their fair share of the bonuses given for winning matches. They are the type who will be the county's representative to the Professional Cricketers' Association, attending meetings in his spare time, reporting back to the players and explaining every last detail about, say, pensions to those who have no idea what he is talking about.

Dale did all those things. In addition he batted in every position between one and seven, timing anything remotely straight through the leg side with his strong bottom-handed grip and closed backlift.

He bowled only gentle medium pacers at county level, but he could 'shape' them nicely away from the right-hander, and on the slow, low pitches of Wales he perfected the art of bowling from wicket to wicket, making him a vital cog in a very efficient one-day bowling attack. In championship cricket he could be invaluable, bowling overs into the wind when no one else wanted to, breaking partnerships that no one else seemed able to.

He was no Jonty Rhodes in the field, but he was no Phil Tufnell either. He was steady, a man to be relied upon.

That encapsulated his cricket. He could always be relied upon. After he retired, the club, on and off the field, kept looking around to see where he was. He was the nuts and bolts that without fuss had been holding everything in place for years, and they were now loosening alarmingly quickly and frequently.

Every side needs someone like Dale holding them together.

Brian Davison

Brian Davison

by David Gower

David Gower played cricket for Leicestershire (1975-89), Hampshire (1990-93) and England (117 Tests, 1978-92, 32 as captain). He is now a member of the Sky television broadcasting team.

Brian Fettes Davison played cricket for Rhodesia (1967-79), Leicestershire (1970-83), Gloucestershire (1985) and Tasmania (1979-88). For six years in the 1990s he was a Liberal Party member of the Tasmanian House of Assembly.

As captain of England, a loose term admittedly, on the day that Viv Richards went happily berserk in Antigua and set the world record for the fastest Test match hundred in 56 balls (a record surpassed, as it happens, by the irrepressible Brendon McCullum on the day I am writing this essay), I can say that I have seen some extraordinary feats of batsmanship in my time.

Viv was himself extraordinary, the best of my era, I would say. How many more words does one need? I was there for most of Ian Botham's legendary knocks, from the 1981 Ashes series through to his blistering assault on Merv Hughes et al in Brisbane in 1986 and then on all sorts of other days when batsmen made the ball disappear many a mile.

However, I want to take you back to The Oval in 1981 and a rain-sodden NatWest Trophy tie that needed two attempts to achieve a result. After two days of crosswords, cards and protracted boredom and all hopes of cricket abandoned, we began a game scheduled to last 60 overs a side, and one Brian Davison belted 137 out of Leicestershire's 261. Surrey's reply had reached 12 for no wicket in eight overs when rain came again and that match had to be abandoned too in favour of a 10-over shoot out.

I opened with Brian, departed off the bowling of the fearsome legend that was Sylvester Clarke for 2 and left Brian to it. His assault began from his first ball and he was particularly harsh on Robin Jackman, whom he immediately hit hard and low for six over extra cover and whose two allotted overs cost 29. 'Davo' would most likely have been man of the recently abandoned match, and it was as if he took it as a personal insult that the rains had interrupted things at that stage. Whatever his inspiration or motive force it worked in no uncertain terms.

His 43 saw the ball bouncing off concrete all round The Oval and propelled us, Exocet-style, to 104 for five in 10 overs, more than enough to ensure victory. The man of the match award was indeed his, and the sad thing is that not many would have seen the innings. Only the hardiest souls would have still been at the ground.

Brian Fettes Davison was born and brought up in Rhodesia and played for his country of birth in South African first-class cricket, as they did then, and for Leicestershire, Tasmania and Gloucestershire.

When I arrived at Grace Road, fresh, in every sense, from the sheltered existence of middle-class England and the King's School, Canterbury, it might have been deemed unlikely that I would strike a rapport with the man ten years plus my senior and from the most different background imaginable. Never before have King's and Gifford Technical High, Bulawayo, been linked in any discernible fashion, let alone featured in the same sentence. And if you think a man whose second given name matches that of a famous Scottish public school would behave accordingly, well, think again!

I arrived at Leicestershire via a wasted year at UCL, from where the only academic figure I recall was Prof. Thomas. He lectured me on Roman Law, rarely if ever saw any written work from me and, when he saw me a couple of years later in the Long Room at Lord's, simply but warmly opined, "I think you made the right decision."

Davo's employment before professional cricket had been in the Rhodesian army during the bloody civil war there. There were some of the most lurid tales one would ever hear from his experiences, none that bears repetition here. It's safe to say that that conflict was not governed by MCC or the Spirit of Cricket, or governed by anything much else in the way of rules, by the sound of it.

As I established myself in the first team it did not take long to realise that he and I shared a sense of humour, daft as it was, and as the years went by more and more shared interests accumulated, again in spite of the contradictions.

He was one of the toughest men you would meet on the county circuit with forearms made of steel and nostrils that flared alarmingly when his hackles rose! If you saw those nostrils go, then it was the sign for those that knew him, friend and foe alike but especially foe, to stand back and give him space. I can guarantee you that on that day at the Oval the flaring would have been in full flow as he walked out to bat that second time!

He was brave in the face of the quickest bowling, brave in the face of any conflict. I, some years later, pretended that trying the Cresta Run a week before the West Indies tour of 1986 was no more than high-altitude, high-speed training, an attempt to pre-empt a cricket ball arriving at 90mph from Messrs Holding, Roberts, Garner, Croft and Marshall. Child's play compared to what he had been doing in army helicopters in Rhodesia.

Somehow he remained fit and strong despite smoking his way through packets of Gunston cigarettes every day. The rate went up before he went out to bat, suggesting that there was a nerve or two to tweak, and he increased the risk factor by ripping the filter off each and every one before lighting up. That's one thing I definitely did not share.

More to my taste was the wine. Despite the Gunstons he had a bloody good nose for wine but the problem was what we could afford. My starting wage at Grace Road in 1975 was £25 a week and it probably had not gone up that much over the first few years. Leicestershire was a county club economically run by Mike Turner, whose skill in balancing the books and, with Ray Illingworth, building teams to win trophies was unsurpassed, but it did mean that the county inevitably came low on the list of major payers!

The Leics Wine Club would have been me, Davo and Martin Johnson, then of the *Leicester Mercury*, since of various national newspapers and now of the *Sunday Times* and still peddling many of the same stories! The rest were always looking for sponsors' tents and a free ale at the end of the day while we at least tried to find a wine list. Sadly the only way to read one in those days was to look at the price alone and take whatever came out cheapest. There was an awful (I use the word advisedly) lot of *Arc de Triomphe!* Thank God things have moved on since then.

People like Davo are not, however, just foolishly gung ho. It takes a strong element of self-preservation and nous to go through all too real army action; and if nowadays wearing a white floppy hat when facing fast bowling seems both outdated and foolhardy, it does not mean that the wearer is oblivious to the danger of 5½ ounces of cork, twine and red leather aimed at his head.

He took it all on, earning respect from all his contemporaries, in county cricket first, then in Australia, where he eventually settled after playing for and captaining Tasmania. Even playing grade cricket in Oz as an overseas player is demanding. One earns respect only by performing with credit and by being a good bloke according to local definitions, which probably involved more beer than wine.

What would have impressed colleagues on both sides of the world was his moral compass. He had a very strong team ethic that underpinned everything he did with all those teams that he represented. In the ranks he would champion his colleagues at all times, standing up for their rights, supporting them with words of encouragement. As captain in Tasmania he would have drawn on all his experience and natural humanity to nurture a developing team, and he led from the front at all times.

That same team spirit and egalitarianism would have driven him, again surprisingly and against the odds, to succeed in his next career, as a Liberal Representative in the Tasmanian House of Assembly, where he would have made some of the more provocative yet reasoned speeches heard, even by Australian standards, in politics. He sat and stood for six years in that Assembly and made an indelible impression amongst the representatives, if not necessarily with an unappreciative electorate who then failed to vote him back in!

The one thing that surprised me about his life in Oz was that he somehow acquired a bastardised Rhodesian/Australian accent and started calling people 'cobber'. I thought he might have maintained that African identity in the face of it all but maybe the desire to be seen to be part of the fabric of his adopted home just forced the compromise.

I always sought him out when we visited, either in my playing days or subsequently with my work with Channel 9 and Sky. Following my tour of India in 1984/5, a successful four months if I might say so, we had to go to Oz to play in what was a sort of mini World Cup in Melbourne. I went straight to Hobart with my girlfriend, Vicki, to stay with Brian and Caroline and chill out for the week we had before preparations for that tournament began.

That was perfect. Unfortunately I had given my team carte blanche to do whatever they wanted for that same week, and seven days and nights in the restaurants, bars and nightspots of Sydney was something that the team did not recover from. You'll be familiar with that word 'momentum', which we nowadays use all too often to assess the course of matches and series. Well, any momentum we had on leaving India had well and truly ground to a halt by the time we played our first meaningless practice match against NSW 3rd XI at Manley and lost.

When I was learning the TV pundit's trade with Channel 9 I found myself in Hobart one night during the 1992 World Cup, hoping I would run into Davo earlier rather than later. Unfortunately it was the latter. Just finishing up after a fish supper on the dock and ready to go back to my bed, I was both delighted and worried that Davo walked in at that moment and by the time we had 'caught up', any ambitions to be fresh, fully fit, firing, bushy-tailed and maybe bright-eyed in the morning were completely scuppered. Especially the bright-eyed bit.

It's like drinking with Botham. It's great fun, highly sociable, involves lots of constant 'rehydration' and is mighty dangerous to your health. And if you are Botham or Davison it does not seem to do as much damage. Having said that there was one night in Taunton before a Sunday League match when Ian saw off the two of us, leaving us to bounce off the walls of the alleys between the Four Alls and the County Hotel. Oh the glamour of it all! The following day as ever Ian was right as rain and first spotted in a bath at the county ground with a cigar and a copy of the *News of the World*, grinning broadly. I was still very green around the gills and even Davo was showing signs of wear. No prizes for guessing who won that day, though it should be on the record that both Gower and Davison somehow made runs.

Anyway, back in Hobart the next morning, I woke to the alarm, sat bolt upright in bed, thought to myself "I'm alive", then collapsed in a heap again to be woken for the second time by Tony Greig saying that they were off to the ground and I should make my own way there. Arriving at Bellerive after the start of play (ooops), I then spotted what looked like a commentary box up a near vertical ladder, climbed it in very unsteady fashion and realised too late that it was the radio box. Both the occupants and I wondered what I was doing there. Descending that same ladder in similarly ginger fashion I wandered off to the media centre at the other end of the ground and found myself next to the great man, Richie Benaud, in my first commentary stint of the day. He was politely bemused that I was now wearing a pair of lurid Bolle sunglasses and remained understanding of my predicament even when Allan Border was stumped by most of the length of the pitch and had made his way half-way back to the pavilion before I, as the lead commentator, managed to find a mumbled word or two to acknowledge what had happened.

I was still feeling a lot less than 100 per cent at the close of play when I was sent for the first time by my producer, John Gayleard, to host the post-match presentation with the captains and man of the match, not a thing of beauty, let alone competence. Of course I have only myself to blame really but then that's what mates are for, to lead you astray in the name of friendship.

The last time I saw Davo is a couple of years ago now at the reunion for the B&H winning side from 1975, a game I watched from the grass in front of the Tavern Stand as a very junior member of the playing staff. At the dinner Davo scrubbed up pretty well, dinner-suited like the rest of us. By breakfast time the following morning after more 'catching up', the stubble on his chin was yet more pronounced and he was sporting a very unpleasant-looking wound on his ankle from a white spider bite back home, visible to all and sundry, and most of us felt like sundry by then, because despite the climate in the East Midlands he preferred a pair of shorts that were showing even more signs of wear than my eyes.

And yet, despite it all, as I talked to him that morning, that indomitable spirit shone through. To me he was always the master and I the pupil. Once a friend, always a friend. My test of friendship is, after months or years have passed, whether or not one can pick up as if no time had been lost at all. Davo will always pass that test.

Charlotte Edwards

by Clare Connor

Clare Connor played cricket for England in 16 Tests and 93 one-day and two T20 internationals (1995-2005), captaining the team from 2000. She is now Director of England Women's Cricket.

Charlotte Edwards plays cricket for England. Up to the end of February 2016 she has played in 23 Tests and 191 one-day and 90 T20 internationals. She succeeded Clare Connor as captain of England.

Charlotte Edwards

She was a well-built girl back then. A diet of home-grown potatoes and a mother whose baking skills were legendary throughout the village had seen to that.

Our paths to wearing the three lions began in remarkably similar ways. Hours of blissful summers growing up at our respective cricket clubs, grass-stained knees, bats in hand, mixing it with our dads and their team-mates, even scoring if there was nobody left to practise with, believing we were 'normal'. We weren't, of course. There were no other six-, ten- or even 15-year-old girls in sight; only reluctant girlfriends clapping their other halves and dutiful wives making the egg-and-cress sandwiches.

Our childhoods were the smells of linseed oil and freshly cut grass, the sounds of the chugging roller and the inimitable sweet thwack of leather on willow. Our dreams were of England glory, of raising our bats at Lord's, of one day being as good as our dads, Steve Waugh and Ian Botham – our heroes.

We were young girls in love. In love with cricket. Pure and simple.

We didn't know each other existed; we didn't know any other girls with the same passion as ours existed for that matter. And then we met each other. She was 12, I was 15. The location for this memorable encounter was the RAF base at Henlow, the slightly random host venue for Junior England trials ... for girls.

This was not what we'd expected. All our coaching sessions, our playing experiences and our dreams were setting us up to play for the England men's team. Of course they were. Because that was our world and we knew no different. All we knew was that we were pretty good at this game played by boys and men. We were the captains of our all-boys' teams and we were amongst the best players. We were wearing the trousers.

Until that day at RAF Henlow when we were both selected for the Junior England Squad. On that day, skirts – or, more accurately, culottes – became our playing attire for the next seven years. It wasn't until 1997 that the England women's team swapped culottes for trousers and our scarred knees could collectively breathe a sigh of relief.

Before the Junior England trial match started, our dads were giving us 'throw-downs' in the nets next to each other. Clive's voice was stronger than my dad's: no-nonsense, but full of love and support: "That's it, Charlotte, well timed, but don't lift your head up too early, stay on it."

I remember how effortlessly she struck the ball, how easy she made it look, and yet how focused she was. Everybody who watched her play for the first time that day knew she was destined for greatness. She was technically proficient, she had all the shots, she had patience and yet she was just 12. It was as if she had been born to play the game.

Fast forward 25 years from RAF Henlow to now, and I'm sitting in the media centre at Newlands, Cape Town. I'm watching Charlotte, or 'Lottie' as the world now knows her, in a T20 international against South Africa. In a few hours' time, England and South Africa men will take to the field. And when the sun goes down on this beautiful ground under the imperious shadow of Table Mountain, it will be Lottie who has been the most capped international cricketer on show today. And it will be Lottie, not AB De Villiers or Eoin Morgan, who is the leading run-scorer in the world in international T20 cricket: 90 matches, 88 innings, 2,403 runs. She's nothing short of a legend.

And what of those years between RAF Henlow and today? There's obviously far too much to tell you in these pages because she has quite literally seen and achieved it all. From her England debut aged 16 when she paid £50 for the privilege of her first England blazer, a maiden century aged 17 against South Africa, setting a new ODI record of 175* in the World Cup in India, still aged 17, to becoming captain of England a decade ago, lifting two World Cups in Australia and England in 2009, winning the Ashes a record five times and most recently turning fully professional for these twilight years of a remarkable career. She has become an institution in our sport.

But, in truth, her achievements transcend our sport. Show me another sportsman or woman with 20 years' international experience and with as much success on the world stage. Show me another leader with as much silverware to speak of whilst also leading a team through the immense change created by the journey from a wholly amateur to a wholly professional era. In 2004, eight years into her England career, she played in the first ever men's or women's T20 international match. She has witnessed the birth of a whole new international format – and she's become the best in the world at it. Show me anyone else in sport who has seen so much change and who has adapted and thrived so brilliantly.

And what of Lottie throughout all of this? Well, I can honestly say that, unlike her sport and her journey through it, she has barely changed. She still talks about cricket with the same infectious passion as she always has. She still hits countless buckets of cricket balls with the same focus, more if anything. She still rings me up on a Sunday to have a chat about batting orders and field placings. Perhaps most endearingly, she still has her roots in those potato fields of home. She loves nothing more than going back to the farm for one of her mum's Sunday roasts and to play with her three-year-old niece.

The little girl who grew up in the cricket club wielding a bat too big for her now has superhero status in the village. But Lottie herself is just the same – despite the CBE, the professional contract, the incessant media requests and the World Cup medals. No airs, no graces, no ego – just a girl in love. In love with cricket. Pure and simple.

Clare Connor (left) and Charlotte Edwards

Anthony Ainley

Anthony Ainley

by Charles Collingwood

Charles Collingwood played cricket for the Sherborne School first eleven and for the Stage Cricket Club. Since 1975 he has been a member of the cast of *The Archers*, playing the part of Brian Aldridge, a fellow Old Shirburnian. His autobiography is called *Brian and Me*.

Anthony Ainley played cricket for the Stage club as well as London Theatres and the Weekenders. A keen sportsman, he also played rugby for Richmond and Middlesex under the name AA Holmes. In a long acting career he is best known as The Master in *Doctor Who*, a part he played for several years in the 1980s. He died in 2004.

Many a county may boast of international players, but what club can boast among its number Errol Flynn, Rex Harrison, C. Aubrey Smith (Charterhouse, Cambridge, Sussex, England – and Hollywood), Jack Buchanan, Boris Karloff, James Mason, Stanley Holloway, Tony Britton, Sam Kydd, Brian Rix and Ian Carmichael? All have worn with pride the red, gold and green colours of the Stage Cricket Club, a club that I had the honour of captaining at times through the '60s, '70s, '80s and '90s.

Captaincy did not come my way for some years. First, I had to put in the hard graft of getting teams together. Ringing round to produce a side for a Sunday or midweek fixture was easier said than done. How well I remember the occasion when the last untried name on my list was H Pinter. Nervously I dialled the number at 8.30 on the morning of the game and, after what seemed an eternity, the receiver was lifted.

"Hello," a deep, husky voice said.

"Is that Harold Pinter?"

"Yes."

With an audible tremor in my voice I enquired whether he would be free to play for the Stage against Richmond that afternoon.

Rather surprisingly without a pause, he said, "Fuck off," and hung up. It was not a great career move, either, as I regret to report that those were the only words the great man ever spoke to me.

My first game as a player – against one of the national bank sides – got off to a good start. The Stage were captained by John Slater, best known as the sergeant in *Z Cars*. I told him I could bowl medium pace, and eventually the call came. "Next over top end, Charles, please," boomed John.

I was taking over from Edward Cast, the lead in the radio soap *Waggoner's Walk*, an older man who had bowled for the RAF at the end of the war. He gave me an encouraging slap on the back: "If you get a wicket in your first over, darling, I'll give you a Spangle." Ted, as he was known, always carried a pocketful of the sticky lozenges to reward team-mates. I'm proud to say he had to give me two Spangles.

The use of the words 'darling' and 'love' were commonplace, and this theatricality frequently unnerved the opposition and could be worth a wicket or two at times as they tried to come to terms with facing a team of luvvies.

After a few years I was elected club captain, which was great fun but not without its pitfalls. Skippering a side of sensitive egos took tact, understanding and compromise. Actors can all too easily be over-sensitive and take things personally. So if someone was bowling tripe and being smashed to all parts and I took him off, it might well end up with him flouncing off to third man, muttering in a stage whisper that he was sure I didn't like him, that I had no idea what he was going through, and that this was the last time he would play when I was captain. Such outbursts were normally short – actors have a need to be loved – so all would be sweetness and light by tea ... hopefully.

Actors do tend to inhabit a world of fantasy. Greeting a new player who boasted that he had kept wicket for Essex Under-19s, then the first time cover point threw the ball in, cried "Ouch!" was bad enough. But worse was the actor who told me on arrival that he had played with Alan Knott and Derek Underwood. I was suitably impressed, only to discover later that it had been on the deck of a cruise ship. When asked to go to mid-off, he turned to me: "Remind me?"

James Ellis, who played PC Lynch in *Z Cars*, was the keenest of cricketers, but his ability and reliability were another matter. Jimmy would only be called up when we were struggling for numbers. He was a renowned drinker and, in order for him to pick up the phone, we had to let it ring three times, then ring off and ring again. That way he knew it wasn't the BBC checking up on him.

His time-keeping was so hopeless that, for a match at 2.30, he would be told it was a two o'clock start. On one occasion, at Putney, it was three o'clock when his car roared up and screeched to a halt. Jimmy leapt out in his whites and raced onto the pitch where we were fielding. As always he apologised profusely for being late, reducing us all to hysterics when he told us he had been lying on the beach that morning in Barcelona when he had suddenly remembered he was due to play cricket that afternoon.

I remember another fixture at Putney when, on a perfect summer Sunday, there was a healthy crowd around the ground, mostly couples and families sitting on the boundary edge in front of their cars. It was my lucky day, the gods were smiling, and runs flowed from my bat. I had scored about 60 when I drove a hard, low six over extra cover which startled and bisected an elderly couple, smashing into the headlight of their car. These mishaps do occur, it's a hard ball, and I continued to bat until I was out in the 80s.

Disappointed not to make a hundred, I returned to the pavilion, took off my pads and sat on the grass to watch the rest of our innings. Sitting with me was William (Bill) Franklyn, a West End and TV smoothie of repute, at that time famous for his Schweppes commercials, each one ending with his catchphrase "Sshhh ... you know who". I remember him asking what he should do about two further ads that Schweppes wanted to film. They had given him a choice: he could either hit Fred Trueman for six and lose to Rod Laver at tennis or be bowled by Fred and beat Rod Laver. As Rod Laver was at his peak he chose to beat him with a flashing backhand pass and to be bowled, neck and crop, by FST.

As Bill and I were chatting, I noticed an irate, elderly spectator advancing in our direction. He stopped and stood menacingly over us. "'Ere, Mr Sshusshussh, Mr Sshusshussh, you broke my headlamp." William tensed but we continued, ignoring him. "Oi, Mr Schweppsy, Mr Sshusshush, I'm talking to you. My headlamp, you smashed it."

I could see the veins beginning to stand proud on Bill's neck. At the best of times he disliked being reminded of the fact that, despite a glittering career, these commercials were what he was best known for. He rose to his feet and proceeded to tell the poor old boy that it wasn't him who had broken the headlight and that, if he didn't go away and stop calling him ridiculous names, it would be more than his other "fucking headlight" he would break. The old fellow fled, and I spent the next few minutes trying to calm Bill down.

By far the most eccentric of the actors in the Stage side was Anthony Ainley, one of quite a number sired by the great Shakespearean actor Henry Ainley. Tony was a fine, strong-looking fellow, sturdy in build with a permanent expression of slight menace about him. Softly spoken, he was the most private of men. A confirmed bachelor, when asked why he had never married, he replied that he disliked the three rings: the engagement ring, the wedding ring and the bickering! Fame had come to him by playing The Master in *Doctor Who*.

We had briefly overlapped at RADA, but it was not until he began playing for the Stage in the late '70s, when he was well into his forties, that our paths crossed again. Never late, he would arrive at the ground already changed and sit in his car having his lunch. As far as one could tell, this consisted almost exclusively of raw vegetables. If one was in favour, an offer of a cauliflower floret might be made.

Tony was a useful opening bat. Striding out, he would be well protected – box, thigh pad, arm guard, gum shield – and proudly wearing his red, gold and green Stage cap, sitting securely atop a full head of false black hair. The complete Irish! It must be said that, when required to field in the slips, if a chance came his way, he could only be described as a one-handed slip fielder; the other hand had to be clamped firmly to his cap.

One season we entered a 20-over evening knock-out competition in London. We were progressing nicely, fancying our chances, when we were drawn to play on a works ground alongside the A40. We began at six o'clock, with the rush-hour traffic in full swing, and as captain I struggled to make myself heard in the field. I was at cover point when the batsman clipped the ball just over the head of Tony at mid-on. Eagerness had led him to creep in closer than I had wanted, and I called across to him, "Tony, stay where I put you!" The din of the roaring traffic forced me to raise my voice somewhat, and he bellowed back at me with the full force of The Master in *Doctor Who*: "If you ever shout like that at me again, you cunt, I'll fucking kill you."

This seemed to terrify the two batsmen more than it did me, and a succession of quick wickets fell. It was, indeed, a 'Master' stroke!

One afternoon I found myself batting with Tony against a promising fast bowler, a 19-year-old county colt. He was a yard or two quicker than Tony was used to, and from the other end I watched as a vicious off-cutter ripped past his defence and, with a sickening 'thwack', hit him smack in the privates.

A great performance followed. Letting out the roar of a rampant bull, Tony flung his bat skywards and fell King Lear-like to his knees. There followed silence. I called to ask him if he was all right. With an unblinking stare, he spat out his gum shield and proclaimed, "You cannot disturb a dead bird in its nest."

Tony died at 71 in 2004, no age at all. In fact, all those I have written about are no longer with us. But the happy memories I treasure of them, and all my other fellow thespian cricketers, will remain with me always.

Long may the Stage Cricket Club continue to produce characters, to be remembered by those that follow as fondly as I do my team-mates.

Wayne Daniel (left) and Vintcent van der Bijl

Wayne Daniel
& Vintcent van der Bijl

by Mike Selvey

Mike Selvey played cricket for Surrey (1968-71), Middlesex (1972-82), Glamorgan (1983-84) and England (1976-77, 3 Tests). He now writes on cricket for the *Guardian*.

Wayne Daniel played cricket for Barbados (1975-85), Middlesex (1977-88) and West Indies (1976-84, 10 Tests).

Vintcent van der Bijl played cricket for Natal (1968-82) Transvaal (1982-83) and Middlesex (1980). Successful in business, he has been South Africa's Manager of Cricket Development and the International Cricket Council's Umpires' and Referees' Manager.

It is nine years now since the three of us sat out in the balmy Barbados night drinking Banks beer and laughing about the good times together. Over the years, I'd seen The Diamond a good few times on my visits to the island in the course of my work and, aside from the shaved head, he was still the muscular man that he had been in in his bull-charge prime, still the same cow-curling eyebrows and chuckle. He'd done well for himself, people on the island told me, invested wisely the money he made from World Series Cricket in the '70s.

I'd seen The Big Fella a few times too, bumped into him in his capacity of cricket manager for ICC, the fellow in charge of umpires and match referees and the decision review system, based in Dubai. He scarcely looked any different from when John Arlott saw him as 'looking remarkably like Lord Longford only not nearly so tolerant'. It was a nice line except the second part: there never was a cricketer more generous to team-mate or opposition.

I was the one who had changed the most, a bit more timber, and shiny head where once there was a generous thatch. And so we three swigged and reminisced about how The Diamond would sit in his chair by the dressing-room door at Lord's, towel round him, waiting optimistically for his latest fancy to call on the big red payphone beside him, so that he could regale us next morning with further detailed tales of conquests made or missed. Then we swigged some more until the bar shut. It was the first time the three of us had been together since the glorious golden summer of the Middle Saxons twenty-six years before. I doubt we shall ever be able to do it again.

Wayne Daniel had joined Middlesex for the 1977 season, a raw 21-year-old who had already played five Test matches for West Indies. Two years previously he had played a handful of second eleven matches for the county, in the first of which he terrorised the Leicestershire dinky-doos to the tune of eight for 54 in the first innings and 12 for 107 in the match. His reputation was already sealed, even before he became a part of Clive Lloyd's grovel-revenge squad the following summer. The Diamond – and this I know – is not familiar with the musical *Oklahoma*, where the wind come sweepin' down the plain – and some poor sap, not him, has to bowl into it. "I'm just a girl who cain't say no," sings the character Ado Annie, and it is a ditty that might be adapted for him: "He's just a boy who cain't bowl slow." There are pace men who rely on rhythm and timing for their speed, all of whom have days where no matter the effort, the ball lacks true velocity. But then there are those, gifted with the brute strength of Wayne, who can muscle it down on good days or bad. Ask him to throttle back, as some might do in the nets on occasion, and with the best will he did not know how.

The Middlesex opener Mike Smith first called him The Black Diamond, for this young bowler was indeed a jewel. He also christened him Rent and Rates, in anticipation of the success that having such a cricketer might bring to the club and thus him. We didn't expect him to be with us all the time. The impact he had made the previous summer pointed to a long and fruitful Test career ahead. We would see him, gratefully, as and when. But then came Malcolm, and Big Bird, Crofty and Patto. Only five more Test matches did he play as he was left in the slipstream of the finest pack of fast bowlers ever to take the field. Between 1977 and 1988 he was to play 214 first-class matches for Middlesex and take 685 wickets at 22 runs apiece, one of the greatest overseas players county cricket has ever seen.

It began many yards back, the ball held in his right hand, hip high, hand pointing down. He pawed the ground, as a Spanish bull might, the first stuttering steps taken on the spot, before breaking into a galumphing heavy muscular stride, a momentum-gathering run, 'whacking thighed' as Dylan Thomas wrote of Myfanwy Price's dream lover in *Under Milk Wood*, until the heaving leap into the crease and a grunting release with a follow-through so robust that his head dipped to waist level and his right hand occasionally brushed the turf.

He delivered what cricketers recognise as a heavy ball, as if it were lead-weighted, more than 5¾ ounces, jarring the bat to send an electric shock up the nerves of the arm with filling-loosening intensity. It came from a heavy length too, seven or so paces from the batsman, back of what might be recognised as a good length, so that the ball was directed at the ribcage. Only for a brief period, from memory, did he deviate from this brutal formula. It became obvious that batsmen were actually driving him straight, a luxury for them that unless his mind was drifting towards his productive social life he rarely allowed. He had spotted that the *Sun* was offering a reward of £500 to the Demon Bowler of the season, the one who hit the stumps most often, and Wayne had his eye on this. We offered to club together and double it if only he would revert to hitting the batsmen instead, and happily he got the message. We never paid out.

Histrionics were not for him. If he beat the bat he was sanguine, a stare perhaps, but then a wipe of a glistening brow and the march back to his mark, moaning about how tough life was having to walk back into the breeze. Just once we saw him angry. He was batting at Hove in the semi-final of what was to be the last Gillette Cup. It was a tricky pitch and Middlesex had been struggling. In those days, the viewing area for teams was on top of the pavilion, square to the pitch, and from here it was obvious that

Arnold Long, the Sussex keeper, was standing a long way back for Imran Khan who was galloping down the hill and bowling with great rapidity. For reasons best known to himself Imran decided to bounce Wayne. It was not a wise move, something instantly recognised by Long, who even before the ball smacked into his gloves was heard to shout: "You twat!" *[NB: Actually it was "cunt", but this is for Arundel!]* The recipient of the bouncer was incandescent when he returned to the dressing room, eyes blazing, the whites turned red. He threatened reprisal and, to the tune of six for 15 from 10 overs, duly delivered. He was utterly brutal.

It is facile to say that Wayne's presence influenced the way in which batsmen played my own bowling, for I'd taken plenty of wickets, and been chosen for England, before his arrival. Indeed, in him becoming the bowler called upon to try and demolish the back end of an innings, he might have cost me quite a few. But there is no getting away from the fact that it was a complementary partnership, valued by myself and the team, not least because having a genuine enforcer adds security to the rest of the side. God, he was good.

With the approach of the 1980 season, though, we thought we would lose him. He was 24 years old now and hitting his prime, in which he was adding nous to his raw uncompromising pace. West Indies were due to tour and, although the famous quartet was firmly established, he had taken 15 wickets at 21 each for Barbados in a team that included Malcolm Marshall, Sylvester Clarke and Joel Garner. Surely he would tour. So Middlesex looked for a replacement, first to the Caribbean, then elsewhere. But those West Indian pacemen who were not involved internationally were already contracted elsewhere – Clarke terrorising for Surrey – while the South Africans Mike Procter and Garth le Roux were playing for Gloucestershire and Sussex respectively. Imran and Sarfraz Nawaz were taken, there were no Indians of any pace bowling substance, Richard Hadlee was in his Nottinghamshire pomp and the best Australians tended not to want to come.

Who came up with the idea of approaching Vintcent van der Bijl, I know not. Not the captain Mike Brearley, that's for certain; he was bothered by the lack of consultation. Although Vince's first-class career had begun before South Africa's years of sporting isolation, he had not played a Test match. But close inspection showed that his pedigree was astonishing: precisely 500 first-class wickets, mostly for Natal, at 17.59 apiece, an average beyond parsimonious. Beyond the fact that he was 32 years old, it almost seemed too good to be true.

It turned out to be an inspirational signing: he was happy to join us for a single year while Wayne would be back the next one anyway. Perfect. And it got better: the West Indies selectors thought that Andy Roberts, Michael Holding, Garner, Marshall and Colin Croft would be sufficient. Wayne was superflous to their requirement and so, through serendipitous good fortune, Middlesex acquired the most potent of all its opening attacks, and one of the most celebrated in the history of county cricket.

It is not stretching a point to say that I played with no kinder person than Vince. He arrived in April, this giant of a man, heavy, and balding so that he carried an avuncular air. This was so obviously a team man. He took me to one side and, as an ice-breaker, quizzed me on the vagaries of bowling with the Lord's slope. He was invariably helpful to all. Beyond all the bonhomie, what we were seeing was a thoroughbred bowler. Hands were rubbed at the prospect.

I would not be telling the complete truth if I didn't say that I was in some ways afronted, not by Vince's presence – how could anyone feel that? – but in the way I felt pushed down the order of things. I was, first and foremost, a bowler for whom the new ball was an important stock-in-trade. It took several seasons of opening with Wayne to convince Mike Brearley of the importance of my taking the first over, rather than The Diamond, in order that I could bowl at least one over before the leather was scarred from his bowling. Wayne didn't bother too much with how the ball landed, just that it did so with maximum impact.

Now, though, not only was I not accorded the first over, it seemed I would lose the new ball altogether. All the overs I've bowled for you, I thought, and you do this to me. Wayne didn't need it in the same way that we two did. Two seasons previously I'd taken 101 wickets. My fears proved not entirely groundless, but we did mix it up on occasions.

If Wayne hustled in to bowl, Vince rumbled, an unstoppable force once he got speed up. He reminded me, bizarrely, of what might happen if an upright piano was being shifted, got loose and started to run down a slope. His was an action in the classical tradition of side-on, his wrist cocked, the ball a marble in his hand. He was brisk, not express but well above fast-medium, and hit the deck hard. I mean really hard. The thing I remember most about it was the noise, the deep 'thump' as the seam hit the ground. At first, he bowled a southern-hemisphere length as he had done all his playing career, just a little too short, so that he beat the bat, got tremendous lift, and the ball thundered through chest high to the keeper. He was beating the bat by too much though, the length wrong for the early season sappy surfaces.

He took five wickets in his first match, a draw against Nottinghamshire, and four in the next, another draw, against Lancashire. Wayne had got himself injured, and I got the new ball back. Through May, and well into June, Vince threatened, but was still a fraction short to be devastating. Then, in the middle of the month, in Middlesex's eighth game, he got it – five for 34, out of eight wickets, against Surrey. As the pitches hardened up and his default length became more relevant, he was devastating.

By the end of that summer Middlesex had secured the county championship and, as a finale, that last Gillette Cup. Vince had taken 85 wickets, with five five-wicket hauls, all at a remarkable average of 14.72 apiece, the lowest season's average he had ever achieved in his career. Nothing will convince me otherwise than that he is the finest cricketer, and certainly the finest bowler, never to have played Test cricket. Wayne had taken 67 at 21.7, with a single five-for, but the force of his personality was always present. My 37 at 32 was a poor return, but there was a consolation five-for against Essex when Vince was absent for a match and I got first over.

I was right down the order now. Simon Hughes was the young thruster, with 18 wickets at 19.5 each. My nadir came at Cheltenham, where I failed to get a bowl on a damp pitch in the first innings as Wayne and Vince shared nine cheap Gloucestershire wickets, and only got some last-resort second-innings overs as fifth change with the surface ironed out to a belter. Mike Procter was well on the way to a match-winning century during which he ribbed me incessantly and humiliatingly.

It is now January 2016, and I am in South Africa, reporting on England's progress in the Test series. I had been looking forward to catching up with Vince in Cape Town. But a few weeks earlier Ian Gould, the keeper into whose gloves the ball thudded so emphatically that summer of 1980, and who had also been there that evening in Barbados, told me that Vince had not been well. I mailed him and he thought he might attend one day of the Newlands Test but his treatment had been debilitating. He was giving up his ICC role. I saw him from a distance, upright and hatted, as he did indeed attend to be awarded a hall-of-fame blazer, but he never made the trip round to the media centre.

Then, a couple of weeks later, while sitting in the press box at Centurion, there was a mighty slap on my back and there was the Big Fella. He was beaming, looked good, and as full of boisterous bonhomie as ever. He was there on business but had made the effort to get round, and it was wonderful to see him. He asked after Wayne. Then, as suddenly as he had appeared, he was gone.

Mark Ealham

by Mark Wagh

Mark Wagh played for Oxford University (1996-98), Warwickshire (1997-2006) and Nottinghamshire (2007-11). A graduate in psychology, he is now a solicitor, specialising in commercial law, with the London-based firm Freshfields.

Mark Ealham played for Kent (1989-2003), Nottinghamshire (2004-09) and England (1996-98, 8 Tests). He is now the cricket coach at The King's School, Canterbury.

Mark Wagh (left) and Mark Ealham

What do you do when a man calls you sweetheart the first time you meet him? Turns out that the best thing is to say hello and sit down next to him. This was my first day at Nottinghamshire County Cricket Club and the start of my friendship with Mark Ealham.

The smallest things can make such a difference. I'm sure that there were plenty of other spots in the dressing room where I could have dropped my bag and my spell at the club would have been just as enjoyable as it turned out to be. But making a home next to Mark, with Chris Read and Dave Hussey in the same corner, and Mick Newell, perched in his office, close by, was a piece of good fortune indeed.

There are a few moments which come to mind when I think of Mark. Firstly, walking out to field in a one-day game against Worcester, all hyped up with music playing and adrenaline pumping following Mick's motivational team talk. I turn to Mark who says: "Oh dear, sweetheart, not sure my hamstrings are going to make it." Then he demonstrates, just about getting his hands to his knees.

Another one-day game, this time against Leicestershire, Darren Maddy bowling to Mark. Mark attempts to drive a good-length ball but only manages to hit it about 100 feet into the air, vertically. He might actually have survived as Paul Nixon, standing up to the stumps, was in two minds whether to catch the ball or let it hit the wickets. It was a slam dunk for Worst Shot of the Year, an award usually picked up by Chris Read; the more swashbuckling members of the batting line-up were always prime candidates. He was rewarded with a heartfelt blast from a puce Mick Newell on return to the dressing room.

Mark was in many ways an old-fashioned cricketer: to borrow from Len Goodman, Mark was a cup of tea in a latte age. He was brought up in a cricketing household, his father Alan playing for, and captaining, Kent. Mark started his career when professional cricket still had much in common with the amateur-led game in which his father had been brought up, and he left with professionalism in full flight. Without wanting to prejudice any futures, it would not be surprising if one or both of his sons continued the Ealham tradition. If they do and the trend continues, their experience of professional cricket will be a further step away from the worlds of their father and grandfather.

*

Team work seemed to take on a new dimension when the Australians dominated cricket in the 1990s and early 2000s. We heard a lot about the subjugation of the individual to the transcendental, unquestionable greatness of the Baggy Green. Legendary tales of the Australian teams which laid the foundations for that success abounded. Parallels between the cricket field and the military/rugby/business worlds were everywhere.

Pre-season was a particularly fertile ground. I have heard talks from the former All Blacks captain Sean Fitzpatrick, a former member of the SAS, a global sailor, and I also spent a week at Sandhurst Military Academy. I loved every one of these opportunities – awe-inspiring, eye-opening, exciting and genuinely inspirational. I will never forget the breathless silence that followed Sean Fitzpatrick's spontaneous one-man Hakka – even thinking about it has the hairs on the back of my neck standing up. Or listening to the never-ending challenges of sailing around the globe with a bunch of people who had never sailed before. Or running through the scrublands carrying a 13-stone dummy on a stretcher with Steve Kirby and others trying to read a map.

But did any of these events make the team any better than it would otherwise have been? I'm not sure.

The team can be greater than the sum of its parts. That is the touchstone, the reason for the promotion of team spirit, the belief that this intangible quality can become a 12th player on the field. But what exactly is team spirit?

I think it is true that under physical exertion the mind gives up before the body; we don't like doing things that are uncomfortable. This makes perfect sense – we need a good reason to push our bodies past enjoyable exertion to a point where it is painful and possibly detrimental. If a person under physical duress would, in isolation, give up, but then remembers his pals or some other cause and pushes on because of that, that is a good example of the effect that other people can have on individual performance. If that person, on the verge of giving up, doesn't give two hoots about his team or team-mates, and his intrinsic sources of motivation are spent, then he is unlikely to put up with a painful experience.

If you are in the military or playing a sport where physical pain is common and 'putting your body on the line' is expected, how you react when at your physical limits is a 'mission critical' factor. When all of your brain's functioning is directed to getting oxygen to muscle, or fear of imminent death is your working environment, I imagine that you need every strand of motivation you can grasp. If the natural reaction is to stop or curl up in a ball, then a clear advantage can be had if some extrinsic factor can make you keep going.

But there is a 'but'. In fact, there are two.

First, I don't think cricket is an activity where this kind of self-sacrifice is needed. I have never been in a position where my life has been threatened on the cricket field in the same way it might be on the battlefield (apart from misfielding when Andre Adams was bowling); I have never been beaten up by the opposition in the same way I might be on the rugby field; and, I think importantly, my performance was always measurable, so a good performance never went unnoticed. Just the normal levels of everyday motivation were required. A pride in performance was important. But nothing that anyone reading this would not recognise in their jobs.

Second, the most important judgement that a coach or captain must make is to select the eleven people who are most likely to score runs and take wickets in the next game. There are caveats and nuances – for example, when investing in the future – but, for the majority of selections, not too much weight should be given to any judgements beyond the likelihood of success in the next game. That is difficult enough to predict.

Nothing hurts team morale more than losing. Winning on the other hand is so powerful that it can bring together a group of people who might otherwise never speak to each other. I've known of teams that couldn't stand each other off the pitch but kept winning. Indeed, some of those teams were reported to have great team spirit!

If the eleven people selected on this basis also have beneficial personal qualities, then a fantastic working environment can be created. But I don't think you can select on the basis of these personal qualities. People are far too complex, in how they will interact with others against a backdrop of sporting performance.

So where does team spirit fit in?

We want to be surrounded by people we like and who like us in return. We want to be well regarded, because we regard them well and value their opinions. We want to do things for these people because we like them. We want to be around them because they make us feel better about ourselves – because they like us. And if we are happy in ourselves and the environment in which we work, then we will perform better. A kick up the proverbial is sometimes necessary, a few sharp words equally, but if they come from a place of respect and concern, rather than being the tip of a deeper dislike, then they can have a positive effect.

This is true in any sphere. Occasionally a rudimentary dislike is rationalised and dressed up in claims about aspects of the other person's personality – selfishness or a lack of desire often the favourites – as to say "I don't like this person" seems to be unacceptable. However, you cannot select on this basis. In my opinion there is no strong evidence that the degree to which the team likes each other causes a better performance on the pitch. Happiness and success are almost always correlated, though, which is why it is easy to attribute causation. If the eleven cricketers who have the highest chance of success in the next game also like each other, then that is an added bonus.

That is not to say that personal characteristics should be ignored. The coach's job in a professional cricket club is to make each individual feel valued, and to promote qualities that allow that individual to perform in their psychological 'sweet spot'. Each has his own sweet spot, so a coach or captain needs to foster a team environment which has enough tolerance to accommodate everybody. Some people, fast bowlers in my experience, need to thump their chest a few times to get themselves 'in the zone'. Others, often batsmen, prefer to have a cup of tea and read the paper to end up in the same place. If either group is not respectful of the other's approach, it becomes more difficult for each group to get into their sweet spot, and that does reduce the chances of success on the pitch.

Full disclosure: I tended towards the cup of tea camp, and it was a constant source of irritation that my approach was seen as a lack of desire. Perhaps, though, I was also guilty of not being tolerant of other approaches.

A team-mate can be invaluable if they identify when a colleague is outside his sweet spot, and pep him up or calm him down as required. But, as even the shortest format of cricket lasts longer than many other sports, such an intervention only has a limited effect; there is plenty of time for a player's mood to change several times over the course of a game. Whilst a team-mate might have an effect for a particular moment, his impact on performance in general is insubstantial compared to success in actually scoring runs or taking wickets. It is the responsibility of the individual himself to ensure that he is ready for the game.

I suppose it is theoretically possible that one person could have such a finely tuned intuition that he could adjust the state of arousal of those around him so that, with him in the team, everyone performed better. However, I have not come across such an individual. A person's runs and wickets are the most valuable contribution he can make.

So for me a good team spirit is one where each player enjoys being in the company of the other members of the team, and where there is room for each player to enter their sweet spot. But there is more to it than just tolerance and empathy. A deep respect for team-mates and the opposition, a desire to explore how good you can be, a pride in performance, a sense of proportion, a willingness to accept responsibility – these are all qualities that make a person a better human being, and therefore a better cricketer.

I don't think you can force these qualities on people. People are complex: they may show some of these qualities to differing extents in different environments. The coach should have his hand on the tiller, gently encouraging these qualities and discouraging less helpful ones. But this is incredibly difficult, and a single person may not be able to do it for all teams, all of the time. Which is why it is helpful if the members of the team are inherently responsible, proportionate and passionate.

*

This brings me back to Mark. To me, he embodied many of the qualities that I would want to promote in a team. He didn't go around banging a drum about how much the team meant to him in the abstract. Instead he competed with everything he had on the field and cared deeply for the people who made up his team. He was often the person people would seek out during difficult times. He was fundamentally kind and willing to give up his time for others.

I'm not suggesting that I would want to play in a team with ten Mark Ealhams, or that Mark was perfect in every respect. But I think it is true that every team that Mark played in benefited from his presence, and that is something of which to be very proud.

Javed Miandad

Javed Miandad

by Paul Parker

Paul Parker played cricket for Cambridge University (1976-78), Sussex (1976-91), Durham (1992-93) and England (1981, 1 Test). He now teaches classics and modern languages at Tonbridge School.

Javed Miandad played cricket for Habib Bank (1975-91), Sussex (1976-79), Glamorgan (1980-85) and Pakistan (1976-93, 124 Tests). He has had three spells as coach of the Pakistan national team and one as Director General of the Pakistan Cricket Board.

In the late 1970s, when I was an aspiring young home-bred batsman with Sussex, the county had on its playing staff four young world-class overseas players: Garth le Roux, Imran Khan, Javed Miandad and Kepler Wessels. The rules of the day allowed only two of them to play for the first eleven at any one time. Sussex, for financial reasons, needed to make a choice which two to keep. I recall being asked by Tony Buss, the county coach, which I would choose. Flattered as I was to be asked, being a junior member of the first eleven, I was acutely embarrassed to be put on the spot in this way. All four would be stunning cricketers in any team, and I knew Kepler and Javed well, as both were inspiring batsmen with whom I had shared a number of formative partnerships in either first or second eleven games.

Imran and Garth already had world superstar status as devastating opening bowlers. Imran had converted from a medium-pace swing bowler in his early days at Worcestershire to an international fast bowler of raw and fearsome pace by the time Tony Greig lured him to Sussex. Subtlety and reverse swing were later additions to his armoury, and his batting was yet to develop its languid elegance and poise. (That said, Imran was always very nervous in the dressing room before going out to bat, and palpably tense at the crease for the first few deliveries, especially, I felt, against good spin bowling.)

Garth le Roux had bowled himself to fame in the second year of Kerry Packer's World Series Cricket. Blessed with an enviable physique, with a simple, aggressive philosophy of bowling fast and straight, Garth had unsettled all the world's best batsmen in that southern summer of 1978/79.

Whom to choose then? Kepler Wessels had always impressed everyone with his ability to accumulate runs, usually from the opening batting slot. His left-handedness, his penchant for trying to get on the front foot and his phenomenal power of concentration and the sheer weight of runs he scored made him the envy of his batting colleagues. True, he lacked the elegance of the emerging David Gower, another left-hander who generated envy, but Kepler's consistency and sheer quantity of runs weighed heavily in his favour. His Afrikaaner provenance added resilience, reliability and resolution.

Javed was the joker in the pack. Not of the same high social class in Pakistan as Imran, he was the street-wise trickster whose brilliance and bravado baffled, bamboozled and buffeted the unsuspecting rank-and-file county bowler, as well as not a few international stars. He arrived at Sussex as a teenager and instantly ran opposition bowling attacks and their fielders ragged, with his jaunty, impish swagger, which seemed only to increase, the longer he was batting. His cheeky smile, directed mostly at fuming opposition spinners, provoked despair in them, and amazement, disbelief, perhaps, and some embarrassment in his own side.

My earliest memory of batting with Javed was in a John Player League match against Northamptonshire at Hove in 1976. It was early July, and I had just returned from my first year at Cambridge University. We were both in our first weeks of playing for the county, batting together for the first time, and not only was it huge fun but it was also formative, especially for me.

The game itself produced very few runs. Sussex scored 141 for the loss of eight wickets in the full 40 overs, a score which seems paltry in the light of the current abundance provided by 20/20 cricket. Northants in reply managed only 121. Under a sunny seaside sky – this was 'the summer of '76' – with the Sussex score on 21 for four, I walked tensely out to the middle to join Javed who had yet to score. I would like to say that we tore into the Northants attack and rescued a dire situation. Not so. Our partnership was worth only 17 runs when I was out for 9, and Javed himself scored only 19 before being caught. But the key thing was that the balance of the game shifted marginally in favour of Sussex during our partnership.

What did take place in the middle was a hugely valuable lesson for me in the art of putting pressure on the fielding side, even in a tense situation. This was done through the stealing of singles, and turning ones into twos, and twos to threes. The remarkable revelation was just how easy this was to achieve. I think my runs were all singles that day. My teacher was the little master, Javed, my peer in age but far more street-wise and savvy at the crease. That sunny Sunday it quickly emerged that we two had an intuitive understanding and, with our natural pace off the mark, we ran the Northants fielders ragged for perhaps twenty minutes.

The key thing about running between the wickets is effective communication between the two batters. Javed, a willing mentor, was able to inspire confidence and was never slow to offer advice. Batting with him later that season in a three-day county match, we were fending off the opening bowlers. With the Hove wicket's natural bounce, much of the time we were set on the back foot. Javed sauntered down the wicket between the overs and said in his cheeky manner, "Paul, sometimes when I play, I not call. Watch my eyes." And I looked at his eyes. "If I go like this" – and he winked with his left eye – "there is run this side. If I go like this" – and he winked with his right eye – "there is run this side." And true enough, in the next over, as the unsuspecting seamer was walking back to his mark, I looked carefully down towards Javed across the 20 yards separating us, and he gave his signature impish grin, and then winked with his left eye. The ball was duly delivered, Javed had already moved on to the back foot and dropped the ball down on the leg side, just in front of where short leg would normally be. With no one there and not a word spoken we scampered an easy single.

This was not an isolated incident; it became an effective and productive liaison between us. Above all, it exasperated and infuriated opposition bowlers and fielders. Fortunately for me, most of the opposition venom was aimed at Javed, who seemed to revel in the attention he gained. It was as if he fed off the challenge and became ever more outrageous in his attempts to unsettle the opposition.

Arguably, our most telling partnership was in the Gillette Cup semi-final against Lancashire in 1978. The game was played in front of a packed Hove crowd who enjoyed seeing two of the most successful one-day sides battling it out for a place in the final. Javed and I enjoyed a fruitful third-wicket partnership of 129 runs in 29 overs, with Javed going on to win the man of the match award for his 75. I remember well the fun we had running some outrageously cheeky singles, which finally exasperated the usually unflappable, sturdy Jack Simmons, Lancashire's miserly off-spinner. On more than one occasion, and with no chance of running either of us out, he took deliberate aim at Javed as he scampered through. One of these shies went for overthrows, and this only illuminated Javed who then turned cheekily and started laughing at the forlorn Lancashire fielders. By now despair and rage had been fomented by Javed in the Lancashire players, but at the other end I felt slight awkwardness at the cheek and bravura of my doughty batting partner.

Batting with Javed was fun. His magical brilliance, his outrageous talent and cheek took the attention from the lesser mortals at the other end. With his jaunty swagger and cheeky grin he took every opportunity to unsettle the bowler. The chief of his tricks was to move outrageously early in his stance as the bowler was in his run. This proved most effective, and provocative, against spin bowlers who sometimes found Javed impossible to bowl to.

I remember a match at Hove in 1976 when Javed tormented the persevering Peter Sainsbury, Hampshire's usually placid and unruffled left-arm orthodox spinner. The bowler's tactic on this occasion was to stop in his run-up when he perceived Javed advancing or shuffling across his crease, and then return to his bowling mark to start his run-up again, no doubt hoping for a more orthodox response from the batsman this time.

Javed had huge fun and persisted in his early movement. In some overs there were three or four false starts. Sussex were chasing an improbable victory. I had been bowled by Sainsbury for 19, and from the boundary I could see Javed baiting bowler and fielder alike, as he guided Sussex to victory with an artful display of batsmanship. He was undefeated on 135 as Sussex cruised to victory with six wickets in hand. This was Javed's first championship hundred, and it was executed with brilliance, panache and some wristy magic.

Peter Sainsbury's bowling figures were pretty impressive – 35 overs, 18 maidens, 65 runs, 2 wickets – and the long duel between the two of them was compelling viewing. John Southern's left-arm orthodox spin from the other end was punished by Javed more mercilessly.

I tried occasionally to imitate some of the less unorthodox of his tactics, especially using my feet to the spinners. What impressed me most about Javed was his ability to get to the pitch of the ball, and to watch it meticulously onto his bat, and then to play with superbly soft hands, the wrists flicking and guiding the ball seemingly effortlessly into gaps on both sides of the wicket. Alternating the strike became very easy – well, it was when Javed faced! The young Javed had flair, vivacity and a joie de vivre on the field of play.

Why do I remember those sunny days of the mid- to late seventies so clearly, perhaps especially 1976? That July not only saw Javed's first hundred for Sussex, in only his second championship match, but it was when I made my debut for the county too. My year on the staff in 1975, playing second eleven cricket, was underwhelming to say the least. In those days Sussex carried a staff of about 25, and often I was not even playing for the second eleven. I felt fortunate to get away from cricket and to start at university in the October. Even more fortunately for me, Cambridge University still played a full first-class cricket fixture list. At the end of June 1976 I returned to Hove, having played all summer on the best batting wicket in England – Fenner's – and in the perfect batting conditions of that hot summer.

I say I returned to Hove, but in fact I was phoned up at Lord's on the final afternoon of the University game against Oxford and told to be ready to be picked up at 6.30 that evening as I was in the Sussex team to play against Yorkshire at Headingley the next day. Thus began my first-class career with Sussex.

It was only a week later that Javed and I were at the crease together in that JPL game against Northants and thus began our county cricket sojourn together. Memories of those days have stayed sharp in my mind.

I regret now not having made more of those few seasons that Javed played at Sussex. We had much fun on the field, and some success, the win in the Gillette Cup final in 1978 being the highlight. But it was also fascinating to spend time with Javed and to get to know, as far as one could, a little about the batting wizard in our midst.

Actually, he was hard to unravel. Part of our interaction consisted of Javed trying to teach me, at my request, a little Urdu, his mother tongue. If only I had paid more attention, or spent more time learning a few more phrases, I might have progressed beyond the banal. The fact is that one focused far too long on trying to improve some tiny aspect of batting in hours of nets and throw-downs, in the long periods when one was not at the crease. This could be days on end in a poor run of batting form! Or time was wasted in idle chatter, and a coffee or two, and maybe poring over a crossword, or the sports pages of the newspapers, mostly not the broadsheets. Those days could be very long!

Some Urdu phrases, however, are still with me, albeit phonetically spelt. *As-salamu alaykum – alaykum salaam –* not Urdu but the universal Muslim greeting – would be our usual morning hello, followed by *Ke aleh –* how are you? *Ti ke.* OK. Heady stuff, but a start. I remember being able to say what we ate for lunch at one time, something like – *lunchme meneh … aloo –* for lunch we ate … potatoes … Well, I thought I could remember ...

While batting, calling in Urdu was common – *ruku –* wait, *jaldi –* quick. *Bohodaja batingi –* well batted. *Bohodaja bolingi –* well bowled. *Easy easy, I take –* not Urdu! – was just Javed when he was in form at the other end of the crease and he wanted the strike. There were a few choice words of insult as well – *banchoot* comes to mind – but these are clearly too crude for the internet at my work-place to let through the filter to allow me to print the translation.

In the dressing room Javed was a lively, chatty, impish personality, fond of little pranks and jokes. He made a clever, very realistic bird noise performed with the skill of a ventriloquist, and he often startled an unsuspecting listener, be it a team-mate, umpire or an innocent spectator waiting in a coffee queue, who would look around in bemused agitation, looking for the source of the tweeting. He often made the noise when he was fielding in the short-leg position. This was usually when Imran was steaming in down the hill at Hove and bowling with pace and bounce, and the batsman would be camped on the back foot. Javed fielded very close and would squat very low in that position, grinning wickedly up at the batsman who was straining every nerve to maintain concentration.

In those early days, on the many away matches, Javed occasionally came out with 'the lads' – Peter Graves, John Spencer and Paul Phillipson come to mind – to relax and to get out of yet another hotel. There was one occasion at Worcester during a three-day county match when we escaped for the evening from the Diglis when Javed allowed himself to be cajoled by us into abandoning temporarily his strict religious code. He did have a couple of pints of the local bitter, but on the next day he was in denial and I never saw him touch another drop of alcohol again, even when the champagne was flowing in the dressing room at Lord's after our Gillette Cup victory in 1978.

Having both Javed and Imran in the same dressing room was fascinating, but I found the relationship between the two off the field difficult to gauge. There was always a distance between them which I used to think naively was because of differences of class. Imran always had the bearing of a prince, being fiercely proud of his Pathan roots and upbringing, while Javed, hailing from Karachi and from a less elevated family background, played the court jester. But the leveller, as happens so often and so wonderfully in sport, was on the field of play. Here Javed, by dint of his huge natural talent and not a little steel and cunning, was regularly elevated, even at that very early stage of his career, to the role of king – the lord of all he surveyed. Imran, too, of course, held imperious sway in this arena.

Thus, in my young and innocent eyes, these two brilliant cricketers were both princes of Hove, and I felt that their combined flair and inventiveness would be the best option for Sussex going into the 1980s. I said as much to Tony Buss when he pressed me to make that difficult choice.

In 1981, John Barclay, in his first year as captain of Sussex, led his young team, spear-headed by the two world-class fast bowlers, Imran Khan and Garth le Roux, to within two points of winning the county championship for the very first time. One-day success followed, too, in subsequent years.

Might it have been different with Javed and Imran? Who knows?

Eddie Hemmongs

Eddie Hemmings

by John Claughton

John Claughton played cricket for Oxford University (1976-79) and Warwickshire (1979-80). He is now Chief Master of King Edward's School, Birmingham.

Eddie Hemmings played cricket for Warwickshire (1966-78), Nottinghamshire (1979-92), Sussex (1993-95) and England (1982-91, 16 Tests). After some years running a village shop in north Lincolnshire, he is now groundsman at Caythorpe Cricket Club in south Nottinghamshire.

Stephen Chalke's recent book on the history of the county championship, *Summer's Crown*, proceeds decade by decade, presenting its statistics by decade. So, if you had been a careful reader of the *Daily Telegraph* during those years and if you thought really, really hard, you might guess that three of the top four wicket-takers in the 1980s were Vic Marks (593), JK Lever (629) and Malcolm Marshall (630). However, I am not sure that many other than close family – and even they might have struggled – would know that the leading wicket-taker of that decade was Eddie Hemmings with 648 wickets. Who'd have thought it? He even played 16 Tests for England in those years.

There is more, much more, to Eddie's tale than this. For all of those 648 wickets were taken after his thirtieth birthday and after he had been sacked by Warwickshire, the county of his birth. Eddie spent most of the 1970s in a fading Warwickshire side, failing first to be the new Tom Cartwright and, later, the new Lance Gibbs. I am not sure that his physical fitness endeared him, even in those more forgiving days, to the Warwickshire authorities and not for nothing was he nicknamed Eddie 'The Whale' Hemmings.

By August 1978, Eddie, although a capped player, had been told, at the age of 28, that his services would no longer be required by Warwickshire so he found himself seeing out his contract in the county 2nd XI, no place for old men, or even sacked youngish men. At such a moment, a man with all his hopes gone can do one of two things. He can, as many others have done: turn up, go through the motions on a variety of deserted club grounds and, a man with no future, watch wearily others who might just have the future that he has lost. Or he can join in. And that's what Eddie did and the rest of us, the young hopefuls, loved him for it.

I have this single abiding memory. The last second team game of the season, in early dewy September, was against Gloucestershire 2nd XI at RAF South Cerney, not an obvious venue for such a match. The grass was already long in preparation for the rugby season, so, when we arrived each morning, the outfield was too wet to start. The general response to this late-season situation was to sit in the tearoom and play cards, but Eddie had a better idea. Each morning, he tied the RAF's rope to the tow bar of his Ford Capri and drove laps round the boundary, roping the outfield.

Why would I remember the make of car unless this seemed a special moment? Our reward was that we won the game and the 2nd XI championship and Garry 'Tight Lines' Thomas and I were awarded our 2nd XI caps and we got drunk on Sambuca in Cirencester.

Eddie's reward for his greatness of heart was more than that. In one of the games before the dewy triumph of South Cerney, we had played Nottinghamshire 2nd XI at Coventry & North Warwickshire Cricket Club and there Eddie, full of energy and enthusiasm, took nine wickets in the first innings. And I have always assumed that it was Eddie's success at that game, and his obvious desire not to go gentle into the end of his career, that convinced Nottinghamshire that Eddie had a future. Which, indeed, he had, as his 648 wickets and 16 Tests proved.

So, that is the strange tale of Eddie Hemmings, but that's not the end of the matter. It leads us to a topic that is too little considered in the history of cricket, the nature of the county 2nd XI dressing room in the 1970s. This is a major omission because the county 2nd XI dressing in the 1970s was a very rich world, and that richness came in many forms.

First, the county 2nd XI dressing room had many other tales to tell, not just Eddie's. In those two cramped dressing rooms there were gathered there 22 people who shared one thing, a lifelong ambition to play professional cricket, the game they loved. And yet, even as Eddie roped the outfield, the Fates were already spinning for them very different destinies.

For some, young players on the county staff with a contract next year and a winter waiting in South Africa or Australia, the match at South Cerney was a time of hope. Nine players in this match went on to play first-class cricket at least a little bit. For others, triallists brought in from club cricket or the Under-19s to make up the end of season numbers, this was a time more of fear than hope. For several players, this match might just have been the last time they ever got within touching distance of their dream. For others, like Eddie Hemmings, South Cerney could have been the end of the road, but wasn't. For others, this match was a small step along the road that would lead to greatness. So, there, amongst the average county players of the future and the disappeared, there lurks, batting at number four for Gloucestershire 2nd XI, BC Broad, who would one day soon find himself an Ashes hero in Australia and produce an even more famous son. But how could anyone have guessed that? After all, he only got 19 and 17 in the match. I got more than that and I caught him at forward short leg off Steve Rouse. What made him so special? It should have been me. It could have been me and that very thought is what makes 2nd XI cricket such an agony. Every player stands on the brink of something.

However, a 2nd XI dressing room was also a place of wonder. Every now and again, through that dressing-room window there was a glimpse of future greatness, in the midst of the ordinary and the mundane. I'll never forget the first time I saw David Gower bat at Lutterworth CC for Leicestershire 2nd XI, or Wayne Daniel coming down the hill at Harrow CC for Middlesex 2nd XI – "He's got a little bit of pace but he's not quick," said KD Smith, to his eternal embarrassment – or a young, innocent and erratic Gladstone Small finding himself at Griff & Coton CC in Nuneaton.

And a 2nd XI dressing room was also a place of infinite difference. It may be that every 2nd XI player shares the ambition to be a professional cricketer, but often that was the only thing we had in common. I don't suppose that Warwickshire 2nd XI was any more diverse than anywhere else in the 1970s, but it was a hilarious, incongruous gathering: Steve Perryman, as Brummie as Brummie could be, whose dad worked – intermittently – at Longbridge, opening the bowling with Richard Le Quesne Savage, Marlborough and Pembroke College, Oxford; David, Tony and Paul Smith, three lads from a Newcastle cricketing family who came on the staff at 16, batting with Robin Ian Henry Benbow Dyer, Wellington College and Durham University.

The contracted professionals, Perryman and Andy Lloyd and Police Constable Geoff Humpage, couldn't understand why the amateurs from public schools turned up only 20 minutes before the game started in their whites. The amateurs, used to cycling to the match at school after leaving period three early, couldn't understand why the professionals turned up at 9.30 and read the *Sun* for an hour.

And then there was Alpheus 'Alphie' Sam, the only cricketer I know named after a Greek river. The diminutive Alphie spent years causing mayhem in club cricket, Midland Club Cricket's version of Brian Lara before Lara even existed. Sadly, Alphie's mayhem didn't quite transpose itself into professional life so he, too, became one of the lost. On the day Alphie got the sack, he batted for much of the day imitating the Michael Holding strut. How we cheered as he strutted off into oblivion – and a life, as the story goes, as a New York gangster.

And a 2nd XI dressing room was not only wondrous and diverse, but also odd. You might have thought that a 2nd XI dressing room would be a place to prepare players for first-class cricket, but somehow that didn't seem to happen much – or not to my knowledge. The matches didn't exist to make us better but were there merely to decide who would be good enough and who wouldn't. It was certainly very unlikely that a senior player, particularly a senior player cast downwards into the pit from the 1st XI, would help or coach a younger one. Why would he? After all, that young player might soon be his successor.

And Alan Oakman, ex-Sussex, ex-England, the man who caught the catches in Laker's greatest match, and 'Coach' to all of us to this very day, didn't seem to do much coaching, except through irony. His job seemed to consist of collecting towels, organising cars and hotels, selling 'coffin' cricket cases – 'a service to the game', as he claimed – and talking over the old days with his similarly employed opposite numbers, like Don Bennett and Doug Padgett.

And, finally, a 2nd XI dressing room was also a place of lies and duplicity, a land of false friendship and esprit de corps. We all might have been pretending that this was a team game, but everyone was also looking around the dressing room, trying to work out who would stay and who would go, who would make it or who would be erased from history.

And yet, after all that, a 2nd XI dressing room was a place of happiness, a land of dreams, and now a land of lost content. What larks we had being paid £6.25 a day plus meal allowance by Keith Cook, the Assistant Secretary, in brown envelopes, staying in one-night cheap hotels in Neath and Newark, playing at Bedworth and Headingley, Old Trafford and BP Llandarcy. And 'Coach' might not have done much coaching, but how we loved him and love him to this day. And whenever the survivors of the 2nd XI dressing rooms of the 1970s meet, how we laugh about Eddie and his Capri – and a thousand other tales. We were happy then.

Tony Lock

Tony Lock

by Micky Stewart

Micky Stewart played cricket for Surrey (1954-72) and England (1962-64, 8 Tests). He also played football for Charlton Athletic and the England Amateur XI. He was England's first cricket manager (1986-92).

Tony Lock played cricket for Surrey (1946-63), Leicestershire (1965-67), Western Australia (1962-71) and England (1952-68, 49 Tests). He settled in Perth, Australia, where he became a coach. He died in 1995.

When I was asked to pen this piece on the outstanding team player I had played with during my career, two names quickly came to mind. They were Tony Lock and Robin Jackman.

'Jackers' was a captain's dream bowler, never giving less than one hundred per cent. He always galloped in with the same intent, no matter whether it was the first over with the new ball in hand or the final over in the extreme heat of a long day.

He made his Surrey debut in 1966 and gradually established himself in the side to the extent that he played a major part in our winning the county championship in 1971. However, in the last match against Hampshire at Southampton, when we needed just six points to carry off the trophy, I made the decision to leave him out of the eleven for a young Bob Willis. The pitch was very dry, and my thinking was that Bob's extra height and pace would get more bounce from it. It was one of the hardest decisions I had to make in my career and, when I told Jackers, unsurprisingly tears welled up in his eyes. However, I reminded him that he had an important job to do as twelfth man and I knew he would do it well, for nobody wanted Surrey to get the six points more than Jackers.

Unknown to me, he had arranged with the umpires that, should we take the crucial wicket to give us the championship, he would bring onto the field a tray of glasses with champagne. The umpires gave their blessing and, although I was – and never have been – comfortable with the exercise, it was typical Jackers. He was Surrey through and through. If ever surgeons have to open him up, I am sure they will find that his heart is in the shape of the county's Prince of Wales feathers.

I joined the Surrey staff in 1953 after completing my two years of National Service, and I was very lucky to begin my playing career in the Surrey side that won the county championship seven years running under the captaincy of Stuart Surridge (for five years), then Peter May (for two). It was the first time that Yorkshire's historical dominance of the championship had been seriously challenged, and Stuart Surridge led the way with a side that contained four outstanding bowlers: Alec Bedser, Peter Loader, Jim Laker and Tony Lock.

Most of the senior players had grown up with Stuey when he had played in Surrey's second eleven and the Club and Ground side, and he was very popular with them when he took over the county eleven. He was a physically imposing figure on the field with his pace bowling and, with a bat in his hand, he was always looking to clear the boundary. However, whilst his statistics in those two departments of the game were fairly moderate, he made himself into a world-class close-to-the-wicket fielder. He was certainly a big inspiration to me to follow in his footsteps.

Stuey was very vocal on the field when directing his troops, and at the same time he was very shrewd in dealing with the different personalities within the senior ranks. He addressed the cool, calm Jim Laker in a totally different way from how he talked to Tony Lock. During Surrey's match against the touring Australians Keith Miller said to him, "Stuey, I wouldn't talk to my dog the way you talk to Locky." But that was his way and a very successful way it was, too.

To Stuey every ball delivered in the match was vital, a contest in itself that we had to win, so concentration from everyone on the field was paramount. When Surrey took to the field in the '50s, some players jokingly likened it to 'going over the top' out of the trenches!

At that time, with the exception of Yorkshire and Wilf Wooller's Glamorgan, none of the counties created pressure through their close catchers in the way that we did at Surrey. Fielding was not taken as seriously as it is now. I remember when I was at school, reading that Clive van Ryneveld's Oxford University side were diving in the field. "Diving?" I thought. "What are they doing?" Then he came over with the 1951 South Africans, and they were all diving around. But there was considerable resistance to it in England. "Oh well," people used to say. "They're from the southern hemisphere. They've got the sun on their backs."

Yet there is no better example of a team working together than when you are in the field. It does not matter how good a batsman or bowler you are; the thing you are going to do most in the game is field. So why not enjoy it?

You can be fielding in the deep, on a dodgy outfield under a red hot sun, in the last over of the day when the bowler has sent down 25 overs and is exhausted. He drops one short, the batsman pulls it away, and you run round, get your chest behind the ball and stop the four. That can give a huge lift to the team.

When I started playing club cricket in Surrey, there were no leagues, so there was not the same importance placed on the result. It was more about testing your individual skills. The enjoyment of scoring runs and taking wickets, and the way that was achieved, were what mattered most. So the atmosphere that Stuey Surridge created was a mile away from my own experience of school and club cricket up to that date.

People I had known from a young age came up to me in my first season and asked me, "How do you enjoy playing in that atmosphere? It must be grim." My reply was, "I love it – because every single ball bowled is vital to the side, and we win!" I had been brought up by a father with a winning mentality, and Stuey certainly had one.

County cricket then was very different from the game today; expectations were different. The Surrey members wanted to see their side successful but, if we were playing Yorkshire or Middlesex at The Oval, a large proportion of them would be hoping that they would be entertained by a century from Len Hutton or Denis Compton. There was many an occasion when we were going down the pavilion steps after enforcing the follow-on when some of the members would call out, "Don't get them out too quickly. I've taken a day off for this."

Nevertheless, Stuey Surridge created the Surrey team ethic where everything achieved was by the team, regardless of the individuals who had scored the runs, taken the wickets or caught the catches. The only thing that mattered to him was the team – so it is not easy to choose one individual as the number-one team-player in that side. But, as I have been asked to, I have chosen Tony Lock who throughout his career – whether batting, bowling or fielding – typified the Team Player.

He was a big, strong guy who delivered his left-arm spin with the mental approach of the quickest bowler in the world. He was at the batsman every ball, and on the bowler-friendly pitches of the 1950s he was at times unplayable.

I was still at school when I first saw him playing for Surrey. He had made his debut in 1946, a week after his 17th birthday. At that time he was an orthodox left-arm spin bowler – although he wasn't a big spinner of the ball; he had a kind of floaty approach and action. This all changed when he was coaching one winter at Alders Store in Croydon. The roof of the net was too low for his flighty deliveries so he changed his action. Not only was his flight adjusted but he now imparted a considerable degree of spin on the ball. The action brought him huge success, even though questions were raised from time to time about its legality. It was said that when he returned to The Oval after his time at Alders, he bowled out the Surrey stalwart Jack Parker, who shouted down the net, "You threw that, Locky."

Some years later, during the match between the Champion County and the Rest of England, Locky bowled out the Rest's captain Doug Insole. With the stumps demolished behind him, Doug stayed still in his crease. "You're out, captain," said the umpire. "I know," said Doug, "but I want to know if I was bowled or run out."

Tony Lock was an incredible wicket-taker on most surfaces and, whilst there were people who said that the Oval pitches were made for him, he took more wickets when playing away than he did at home.

It was in 1959 that he saw himself bowling on film for the first time. It was in a cinema in New Zealand at the end of the tour to Australia. It was said that he was in tears back at the hotel and vowed to change his action again. He switched to having his bowling arm coming in from behind his back in a long sweep, something akin to the way Johnny Wardle bowled. However, he felt that he could not impart the spin he wanted with this method – in spite of taking over 100 wickets that summer. The next summer he changed again to a more orthodox method with his bowling hand coming up in front of his chin and then over in a complete arc, and he took 100 wickets again. I don't know of any other bowler who has taken 100-plus wickets in three consecutive summers with three different actions. Incredible!

Locky would miss the odd match with a damaged spinning finger. I say 'damaged'; the flesh of the forefinger on his bowling hand was split to the bone. It was horrible to see and would be mended by friar's balsam which he poured onto it liberally. How many spin bowlers today split their spinning finger?!

In 1963 Tony Lock emigrated with his family to Perth, where he was the first bowler since the war to take 50 wickets in a Sheffield Shield season. He captained Western Australia to the winning of the Shield, the first time the state had achieved this in a full season of matches.

Locky could bat, though his statistics are not that impressive. He could strike the ball in orthodox fashion as well as with a more agricultural method, and he could defend. He never put three figures on the board; his highest score was 89 in his last Test, against a formidable West Indies attack.

Where Tony Lock came into his own was in the field where he always seemed to be in the game. Although he would begin the day in immaculate whites, in no time at all he would be covered in grass and dirt stains from an early dive for a brilliant catch or a stop at leg gully or leg slip – and, when bowling, he would be diving around after every caught-and-bowled.

In spite of all the diving, I thought some of his best catches were those going at the speed of light round the corner at short leg. He was absolutely brilliant, and he knew it. If I caught a useful catch at short square leg, he would come racing up to give me a hug and a kiss, covered in dirt and sweat, saying to me, "You are the best short leg in the world," then adding, "in front of square."

It is a privilege to say I played in the same side as Tony Lock. He took nearly 3,000 wickets and caught over 800 catches, but most of all he was a real Team Player.

Richie Parker (left) and Andrew Wingfield Digby
outside the Swan at Swinbrook

Richie Parker

by Andrew Wingfield Digby

Andrew Wingfield Digby played cricket for Oxford University (1971-77) and Dorset (1972-92). He is now vicar of St Andrew's Church in Oxford and plays cricket for the village of Swinbrook.

Richie Parker plays cricket for the village of Swinbrook where he is also the groundsman.

Swinbrook Cricket Club in the Cotswolds is where Richie Parker plays his cricket.

This is the club I am privileged to play for most weekends. Bordering the ground to the north is the River Windrush and just beyond it the Swan Inn with its Mitford sister memorabilia and pictures of Mr Cameron hosting M. Hollande to a typical pub lunch. In the east is the road down from the A40, the wooden pavilion is on the south side and a splendid row of poplars guards the ground from the prevailing westerly winds.

Richie is a big man. He drives the local skip and is the best sort of village cricketer. He bowls little cutters cunningly, hits the ball out of the admittedly small playing area repeatedly and drops a vast number of catches. He prefers to take the new ball and bowl into the prevailing wind. This means the road with its occasional passing traffic is behind him. I have only ever seen him bowl from the road end. He was not born yesterday. I have to bowl with the poplars behind me. Nobody else gets choice of end when Richie is playing. And since he is always playing, unless he is having one of his periodic pre-retirement melt-downs, we bowl the other end.

When Mike Atherton decided to write about village cricket in *The Times*, a subject about which I suspect he knows very little, he needed a picture of a typical English village ground. Rather to my surprise, but much to my delight as I opened *The Times* that morning, I saw a splendid photograph of Swinbrook Cricket Club near Burford

Richie has been part of Swinbrook CC for a very long time and I am a relative new boy so I sought help for this chapter from his long-time team-mates. I realised quite quickly that my subject has attained a legendary reputation over the years. At university I studied history, majoring in American history as there is so much less of it and it gave me more time for cricket. I became very enthusiastic about Abraham Lincoln and, as all students of Lincoln will know, distinguishing legend from truth in relation to him can be difficult. The same can be said of Richie. He has batted in every position in the order and no one questions that he has hit the biggest six ever seen on the ground. Most of the opposition teams – well, those of a certain age – greet him respectfully before every match. He is spoken of in tones of affection and respect in club bars throughout the Cotswolds. Perhaps two stories will give you a flavour of my team-mate.

While league cricket on Saturdays is our meat and drink Swinbrook is also a popular venue for touring teams. Regular visitors include the Private Eye team founded by Willie Rushton, known as Lord Gnome's XI. Willie by all accounts arrived by helicopter – a large one, I assume. Richie loves playing touring sides; he enjoys the banter but also likes to pitch himself against some better players than we habitually meet in the league. Whether Willie would come into that category is uncertain!

On one famous occasion Swinbrook needed seven to win off the last over with eight wickets down. Richie was not out quite a few at the non-striker's end, while our other club stalwart, Vic, was about to face his first ball. Sensibly Vic nurdled a single. The game was surely safe as our hero had strike. Solemnly he then proceeded to block the next four balls. And when I say block, I mean block. Richie is a man of substantial frame and his block is a massive defensive statement. As you might imagine he does not trade in short singles. Several times during the over Vic approached him and suggested a more attacking approach. Lord Gnome's rapid opening bowler was confident that a draw at least was secure as he approached for the final ball of the match. Richie had shown no visible sign of attempting victory.

They are still looking for the final resting place of that ball. Richie smote it clean over the pavilion, over the old Burford Road and into the President's garden ... Swinbrook recorded a famous victory.

Another regular visiting team was the Scott's XI, named after the great explorer; they claimed to have played on every continent including the Antarctic. These were formidable opponents for a Swinbrook Sunday team, who met as usual for their warm-up in the Swan. Ten minutes or so before the start Richie emerged from the pub with his team, crossed the river bridge and approached the ground where an amazing sight greeted him. The opposition were to be seen either jogging around the pitch or engaging in various stretching exercises. The blood drained from the faces of the youthful and mildly inebriated Swinnie Sunday part-timers. However, Richie was not to be outdone by this impressive preparation. Without hesitation he gave his pre-match talk to his intimidated team: "Back to the pub, lads" ... and off they went.

There is much talk these days of the 'spirit of cricket'. Professional players would be aghast at the behaviour of some teams in the league; professionals are often expert sledgers but rarely resort to open abuse of umpires or to threatening violence to opponents.

There is talk at MCC of yellow and red cards being given to umpires as they are to referees in football. This is an appalling thought. The marvellous chaps who bother to turn up to umpire in the fourth division of our league would, I suggest, be out of their depth with such powers. Little Ayotollahs could be created overnight. Better behaviour on the field can only be secured by captains controlling their players and the senior players in every team setting a culture which enables a good game to be had by all, even if the umpires get things wrong.

The umpires know they will have no dissent from Richie. He has learnt to take in his stride the rough and smooth of fourth-division umpiring in the Oxfordshire Cricket Association League; he turns his back quickly on any opponent who mouths off. A village cricket team dressing room is a gathering of people from all sorts of backgrounds. The local squire hangs his jock strap on the same hook as his gamekeeper. In our team we even have three descendants of WG Grace himself – the Three Graces. But Richie sets the culture of our team, and there is never any trouble.

There is much more to Richie than just being a fine player. He is also our groundsman, and hours and hours are spent preparing pitches in what is frankly an unpromising field. We are very close to the river. On one occasion the rather tidy figures of my first few overs were wrecked by a big hitter who hit me first into the river, then into the nettles beyond the river and then into the pub car park – well, nearly.

We flood easily. Others in this book may describe wickets they bat on as 'roads'. Suffice it to say that 'Swinnie' is never a road despite Richie's best efforts. I have played on hundreds of cricket grounds in my career, and I have never encountered a wicket quite like Swinbrook's anywhere else in the world. It defies description really but, if you can imagine 'slow and unpredictable', you will be getting the idea. Amazingly I am sometimes asked to open both the batting and the bowling (Richie, of course, gets the first over from the road end). Let me just say that it is always rather good news when the skipper tells me we are bowling first.

Richie would not claim to be a qualified groundsman but he has a countryman's feel for the land and the ground always looks a picture. I can think of no better way to spend a summer's evening, having been dismissed for my customary solid half dozen, than, pint in hand, with the sun streaming down, watching Richie Parker knock off the runs for another league victory.

Graham Gooch & John Emburey

by Simon Hughes

Simon Hughes played cricket for Middlesex (1980-91) and Durham (1992-93). His book *A Lot of Hard Yakka* was the William Hill Sports Book of the Year while on Channel 5's cricket highlights he has established himself as The Analyst.

Graham Gooch played cricket for Essex (1973-97) and England (1975-95, 118 Tests, 34 as captain). His combined aggregate of runs in first-class and one-day cricket is the highest in the history of the game.

John Emburey played cricket for Middlesex (1973-95), Northamptonshire (1996-97) and England (1978-95, 64 Tests, two as captain). He was Middlesex coach from 2001 to 2006.

Graham Gooch (left) and John Emburey

I never really had a close friend amongst county cricketers. It was probably my fault. I was too erratic. I did have England's assistant coach Paul Farbrace as a lodger in my London house for a few months while we played for Middlesex, until he couldn't stomach my chaotic lifestyle and mad friends any more.

The closest in terms of lifestyle was probably Gloucester's Phil Bainbridge. We played together during Durham's first two years in the county championship and had a similar relaxed view of the world, sense of humour and inability to go to bed at a reasonable hour. It was therefore a mistake to share a house in Darlington, since we were generally coming in only a short time before our other housemate, Paul Parker, was waking up – he liked to strum his guitar from about 6am. So the relationship did not help our cricket one bit. No wonder we were bottom of the table those two years.

One of the most enduring friendships that I was aware of on the county circuit was that between two arch opponents, though they were united when playing for England. John Emburey, Middlesex's stalwart off-spinner with a high level of professionalism and a dry sense of humour, was magnetically attracted to Graham Gooch, Essex's master batsman. The feelings were mutual. In fact, they had been virtually inseparable ever since they roomed together on the London Schools tour of East Africa in 1969.

They shared many characteristics: a working-class discipline, a phlegmatic temperament, an affection for South Africa, and a slightly thin speech habitually laced with expletives. Emburey once answered a reporter's off-mic question about his back injury with, "Well, to be honest, the fackin' facker's fackin' facked!"

Mork and Mindy, Ian Botham called them, because of their unique friendship and the strange, unintelligible language they spoke. Gooch affectionately referred to Emburey as 'Ern' or 'Knuckle' (a South London version of 'mate'); Emburey called Gooch 'Gray' or 'Zap' (alluding to his Mexican moustache). During county games Emburey spent so much time in the Essex dressing room playing bridge or chatting with his old mate that we actually dumped his gear in there on one occasion.

They were diametrically opposite in physical terms, however. Gooch only had to look at a cream bun to put on weight, so he adhered to a rigorous fitness routine. He was mystified by Emburey's apparent lack of enthusiasm for practice and training, and on one of their early tours together he asked him, "Well, how d'you keep fit, then?"

"I go bed early," *[sic]* Emburey replied.

They mimicked each other relentlessly in benefit matches. Gooch would bowl round-arm with a towel stuffed down his front; Emburey stood at the crease with an exaggerated backlift and wobbling head. Their laconic exchanges at slip in charity games were priceless.

"Anything lined up for this winter, Ern?" Gooch asked during their ban from Test cricket.

"Oh, I think I might work in computers," Emburey mused.

"What you gonna do, paint them?" Gooch retorted.

Gooch seemed the dominant partner in the relationship, and the more dedicated, and, although there was mutual admiration, he usually milked Emburey's bowling with such ease when Middlesex played Essex that it was pointless putting him on. Emburey had even tried one year to get Gooch plastered on red wine so that he couldn't bat the next day. The plan misfired. Set an unlikely 214 to win after tea, Essex cantered to victory in 31 overs. Gooch, playing almost in a trance, lashed a brilliant century despite Emburey inciting Daniel into a ferocious spell of bowling.

What they recognised and respected in each other was an unshakeable resolve and consummate professionalism on the pitch and a wonderfully phlegmatic temperament. They were both indefatigable in a crisis, and could disperse tension as effectively with a funny comment as with an influential act. Gooch used his wit to great advantage. He had an infuriating ability to laugh and joke with the bowler while he was non-striker, sympathising with the footholds or the strong headwind or the pernickety umpire, then ruthlessly larrup the poor, unsuspecting chap – me – all over the park when he was back at the business end.

Ultimately they were united by their love of their game and their commitment to a cause. They still care passionately about England's fortunes. Gooch finished his career with a far superior record, of course, but Emburey was the rock of the Middlesex team and an unheralded star of the 1980s who can still be relied on to provide a mean spell in a benefit match, even in his sixties.

Both men can talk the hind legs off a donkey. The good thing, though, is that both love chatting about cricket. It is a dying art. Talking incessantly about cricket might have killed a few marriages, but it is such a valuable way of learning about the game. The source of my role as The Analyst came from listening to observations Emburey made, discussions we would often have and small adjustments to his field when bowling to different batsmen, even in benefit matches.

Gooch and Emburey may have made a few enemies when they went on the 'rebel' tour to South Africa – they were both banned from international cricket for three years – but they were not well paid at the time and were disillusioned with the way English was cricket was run. And it was a perfect arrangement because they could play together for Western Province in the winters until the ban was complete.

Living in beautiful Cape Town, playing in a phenomenally high standard of domestic cricket (one Currie Cup game a week), a bit of golf, some wine tasting, jogs on the beach (Gooch), barbeques and long evenings of cricket chat. I'll bet they'll say that, despite the Ashes wins and all their other achievements, those were the best years of their lives ...

Jack Simmons

Jack Simmons

by David Lloyd

David Lloyd played cricket for Lancashire (1965-83) and England (1974-75, 9 Tests). He coached Lancashire and England and, as 'Bumble', has developed his own highly popular style as a commentator on Sky television.

Jack Simmons played cricket for Lancashire (1968-89). A successful businessman, he served as chairman of Lancashire (1998-2009) and chairman of the cricket committee of the England and Wales Cricket Board (2008-10).

Jack Simmons joined Lancashire very late in life for a professional cricketer. He came into county cricket at the age of 29 after playing for a host of clubs around the Lancashire leagues. During his time at Lancashire he developed into a genuine character and never lost his amateur ways.

In Jack's first Roses match we batted first and had a particularly good morning session, scoring well over a hundred runs without losing a wicket. This was particularly satisfying for us as we had been on the receiving end in recent games against Yorkshire. Our captain, Jack Bond, wanted to keep the momentum going and to continue the good work. He called all the troops into the dressing room after lunch to fire us up for the afternoon session, but only ten turned up. 'Simmo' was nowhere to be seen.

They searched all the usual places: toilet, snack bar, physio's room. Eventually our scorer, 'Mac' Taylor, tracked him down in the closed-circuit TV monitor room, headphones on, racing paper open, listening to the 1.45 from Wetherby. Mac said that he thought Jack ought to report back to the dressing room as the captain had just got all the lads together for a little meeting.

"Tell 'im I won't be long. I'm just listening to this race. I've got a tenner on t'favourite."

Jack was never too thrilled with pre-season training. The diet was always starting tomorrow; the leg always played up a bit which prevented any running. Oh, and he was thinking about packing up smoking.

We used to finish our morning sessions with a three-to-five mile run around Chorlton and Old Trafford. Simmo knew every short cut there was. He was spotted in various places which bore no resemblance to the route we were supposed to take. He was seen alighting from an articulated wagon at the gates of Old Trafford, having flagged the driver down and told him he was lost. He was also seen slumped in the doorway of the Throstle's Nest pub suffering from an acute stitch.

On another occasion he set off on the run with the *Manchester Evening News* under his arm. The reason for that was that he had seen one or two houses for sale in the area which he thought he might buy and change into flats to rent out to our players who lived well away from Old Trafford, or to triallists and visiting spectators!

Jack's locker was like a miniature office. One day there were papers, bills and invoices strewn all over the place. Steven O'Shaughnessy asked if he had lost something. "Aye," said Jack, "I've put thirty grand in an account and can't find it anywhere. Anyway, somebody will send me in a statement and then I'll know where it is."

Steven was perhaps the last person to say this to as he had just come off the telephone after trying to persuade the bank manager to advance him £200 to buy a car. He went out of the room scratching his head and muttering, "He must be playing a different game from me."

Simmo was the king of the complimentary tickets. We were only allowed two per game, but Jack used to conjure them up from all over the place. He didn't have the heart to tell people, "No, I can't get you any." But he expected the same treatment when he wanted tickets for himself.

We were rained off during a day at Chesterfield. Simmo had seen in the local paper that the Tremeloes were appearing in cabaret at the local Palais. He rounded up the lads, ordered the taxis and took us down to the gig. There was a fair crowd gathering with quite a long queue. Jack marched up to the pay kiosk and informed the young lady that Lancashire County Cricket Club had arrived. "Would you like to join the queue?" the bemused girl said. "It will be one pound each."

"No, you don't understand," said Jack. "It's Lancashire County Cricket Club. That's Clive Lloyd over there with Barry Wood, Frank Hayes and the rest of the team."

"I'm sure it is, sir, but would you mind joining the queue? It's one pound each," she repeated.

"No, no, listen," said Jack. "When your lads come up to Manchester, they get comps to get in places, and it should be the same for us down here. We should get in for nowt."

The young lady had had enough by this time. "I'm sure you should," she said, "but this is one place where it's one pound each to get in."

"Right," said Simmo, leaning into the kiosk. "Wait till you want some Gillette Cup tickets. Don't come to me for 'em."

Some joined the queue, some went back, leaving a rather bemused young lady wondering what on earth the Gillette Cup was.

The lads would always be looking to take a rise out of Jack. Graeme Fowler in particular. In one match at Old Trafford Jack batted particularly well and practically won the game single-handed. He got a terrific ovation from the crowd, and all the lads mobbed him when he got back upstairs.

'Foxy' Fowler told Jack that the lads had decided to make a presentation to him in view of him playing so well. It was something that Jack would find extremely useful, he went on to say. Jack eagerly took off the brown-paper wrapping and there it was, the ideal present for Simmo – a toilet seat with the following items strapped to it: a packet of fags, a box of matches, a telephone, the *Sporting Life* and a can of lager!

Jack's appetite is legendary and not without good reason. After all, he has had one delicacy in a local chip shop named after him on the menu. It is the imaginatively named 'Jack Simmons Special', consisting of pudding, chips and peas with a fish on top. It is known as *nouvelle cuisine* in Great Harwood where Jack lives.

On returning home from an away fixture late one night Jack asked me to drop him off at his favourite chippy. He ordered one of his famed specials and then sat on the wall outside and proceeeded to demolish the lot.

"Why don't you take them home and eat them there?" I enquired.

"No," he said. "If I did that, Jacqueline wouldn't make me any supper."

Once, during a game at Blackpool, he booked a table for four at Morton Fisheries, which is a sit-in chippy about a mile from the ground. So what, you may ask. What's so special about that? Well, he booked it during the lunch interval!

Lancashire were fielding, and Jack led the charge off the field. He and his fellow diners, Clive Lloyd included, drove off to the chippy in their cricket gear and got stuck in. Jack had the 'usual': pudding, chips and peas with a fish on top. The customers couldn't believe that part of the team were away from the ground and dining in style, so to speak.

One chap watched Jack demolish his plateful and, with a smile on his face, said, "If you can eat that lot again, I'll pay for it."

What a challenge for our hero! He set to again and polished off another special. On the way back I think it was Clive who said, "Simmo, you must be full to bursting."

"I am," replied Jack, "but I wanted him to pay up. I know him, he's a tight bastard."

There was another occasion at Liverpool. Lancashire were in the field, and Jack was giving frantic signs to the dressing room from his position at second slip. What was required? Was it tactics, a shrewd field change, another sweater or maybe a stud had come loose? John Abrahams, our resident twelfth man at the time, ran out, spoke to Jack and came back, doubled up with laughter. "You'll never guess what he wants," he said. "He wants a pencil and paper so that he can go round the fielders, umpires and batsmen to take a lunch order for fish and chips because it's always a salad here. He says only rabbits can live off that stuff!"

In a game at Trent Bridge – I think it was during Clive Lloyd's reign as captain – we had Jack fielding at widish mid-off which meant he would have quite a long chase if the ball was driven back past him. Sure enough, a well-struck half-volley was despatched just beyond Simmo's reach. Our hero tramped off after it and caught up the ball just inside the boundary rope. At this stage the batsmen had run a leisurely three. As Jack stopped the ball a wag in the crowd shouted, "Come on, Simmo, you big, fat bastard."

Clive bellows after him, "Hey, man, what are you doin' down there?"

"He's just called me a big, fat bastard."

"Well, you are a big, fat bastard," says Clive. "Just throw the ball back; they've run five already."

A similar situation arose in a game versus Glamorgan, only this time it was not a spectator who offended Simmo. It was one of the opposition players – none other than Javed Miandad.

Jack was bowling a tight, economical spell and had tied Javed down for the first five balls of an over. Javed pushed the sixth ball into the off side and threatened to run. Jack was onto it as quick as a flash and stood with the ball between his feet. Most players would have retreated into the crease, but Javed stood his ground about five yards down the track. The umpire, quite rightly, didn't call over as he anticipated further developments. He wasn't disappointed.

"Come on, fat Jack, throw the ball," goaded Miandad.

Jack was affectionately known throughout the cricketing world as 'Flat Jack' because he bowled his off-spinners quick, with a flat trajectory. I am sure that Javed knew this and deliberately called him 'Fat Jack'.

"Who are you calling 'Fat Jack', you sawn off little bastard? Get back in that crease."

Javed didn't. He kept inching forward, and Jack bent lower towards the ball. All of a sudden Simmo swooped and hurled the ball at the stumps. Unfortunately he missed and, more unfortunately, Graeme Fowler, our wicket-keeper, also missed. In fact, he wasn't even there. Peter Lee, who was fielding in the deep square leg area where the ball was heading, didn't see it either. He was moving towards his run-up and taking his sweater off.

The ball careered over the boundary rope and into the advertising boards. The umpire duly signalled four and called the end of the over.

Again Clive Lloyd was the captain: "What's goin' on here, man?" he shouted. "What are you trying to do?"

"I'm trying to run the bastard out," replied Jack in a rather threatening way.

'Foxy' Fowler couldn't stay out of this for long and came in with: "I think he's trying to get you riled, Simmo."

"Yes, and he's bloody well succeeded," said Simmo as he proceeded to kick his cap all the way to second slip.

Andrew Lloyd Webber (left) and Tim Rice

Andrew Lloyd Webber

by Tim Rice

Sir Tim Rice plays cricket for the Heartaches, the club he founded in 1973. An award-winning lyricist, he collaborated with Andrew Lloyd Webber in the writing of the musicals *Joseph and the Amazing Technicolor Dreamcoat*, *Jesus Christ Superstar* and *Evita*.

Andrew Lloyd Webber has no interest in cricket. A composer and impresario, he has written the music for many productions, including *Cats* and *The Phantom of the Opera*. He now sits in the House of Lords as The Lord Lloyd-Webber.

Having founded and run a private cricket club for almost half a century, Heartaches CC, I have accumulated quite a few team-mates over the years. It would be a grave injustice to all the others were I to single one chum out for inclusion in this distinguished tome. So I hope it will cause no editorial ructions if I write about a team-mate who has virtually no interest in cricket whatsoever. However, he was persuaded to compose a score for an oratorio with a cricketing theme, despite the fact that he has never heard of Ian Botham or Michael Atherton, let alone Joe Root. However, they have certainly heard of him – for his name is Andrew Lloyd Webber.

Yes, Andrew and I, theatrical team-mates, have had a go at portraying aspects of the world's greatest game in musical form. We were, of course, by no means the first to take on this challenge. One notable predecessor was *The Batsman's Bride* (1957), a delightful 50-minute operetta, with music by Percy Heywood and words by Donald Hughes, two Welsh schoolmasters. Cricket in music has a long and distinguished past, best recalled in the late David Rayvern Allen's wonderful book *A Song for Cricket*.

Our work was commissioned for a private event in the summer of 1986. I might as well name-drop thirty years later. The private event was a party at Windsor Castle to celebrate HM The Queen's sixtieth birthday, and we were commissioned by Prince Edward, who at the time was working for Andrew's theatrical production company, the Really Useful Group.

A mere half-hour of sparkling entertainment was required. To my surprise, bearing in mind his extremely limited cricketing horizons, Andrew was more than happy to go along with my suggestion of a tale of love and romance behind the sightscreens. He came up with a fine collection of extremely catchy tunes. So catchy, in fact, that many of them have surfaced elsewhere since, in various extravaganzas that have spanned the globe. Even today whenever I hear the anguished cry of the Phantom of the Opera, contemplating his miserable fate via one of ALW's great ballads, I can only imagine him facing the beamers and bouncers of Winston B Packer, the demon fast bowler of *Hearts and Wickets*.

When our cricketing creation was first performed its title was simply *Cricket*, a rather unimaginative title, which must have been chosen to match the also rather unimaginative title of my other project at the time – a show called *Chess*. I now prefer to refer to *Cricket* by the more romantic name of *Hearts and Wickets*. Whatever its appellation, the show packed a lot of action and romance into its thirty minutes. As was the case with *Chess*, it was important to come up with a storyline that had a chance of appealing to those who shared Andrew's view of the sport.

The action takes place at the beautiful cricket ground within the borders of the Earl of Headingley's country seat. It is a hot, bright afternoon in June and the Earl's team have just begun their innings. Our hero, Donald Hobbs, the home side's number four, is next man in. The score is 23 for one. The Earl and his team sing of *Bat on ball – the manly thwack of blade on leather* during which opening number another wicket falls and Donald strides *bravely to the crease*, watched

> *bravely from the boundary ropes*
> *a sweet English rose whose hopes*
> *stride out there with him.*

This is Emma Kirkstall-Lane, the Earl's daughter, Donald's bethrothed.

The Earl is worried that Emma doesn't seem to be gung-ho for Donald's cricketing prowess. This is a vital match for his team. Indeed, the old buffer's fears are proved to be justified as Emma sings 'The Seasons Slip Fruitlessly By', in which she reveals that

> *Love seems less important to my lover than his scores*
> *From April to September and for longer if he tours.*

As she sings, Emma is unaware of the nearby presence of a rather common form of life, a racing man, Vincent St Leger.

The foul Vincent, having heard Emma's heartfelt outburst, slyly suggests that she takes up the Sport of Kings – *You can't compare a cricketer for breeding with a horse.* After fewer than sixteen bars of reflection, Emma decides to change her life, tears up her scorecard and runs off with Vincent.

Meanwhile, Winston B Packer, the visitors' lethally fast West Indian bowler, lets Donald have it, via a vicious reggae-tinged aria 'The Art of Bowling', interspersed with cries of pain. As wickets fall around him and his injuries mount, Donald notices Emma leave with Vincent. Should he sacrifice his wicket and sort out his private life, or stay in for the team's sake and try to win the game? In the show's big ballad he sums up his dilemma:

> *Since flannels first were worn*
> *Has any batsman borne*
> *The strain of losing his intended*
> *While facing vicious pace?*
> *Would Bradman, Hobbs or Grace*
> *Have left the matter unattended?*

He comes to a magnificent conclusion:

> *My choice is Hobson's now*
> *Do I bat on, allow*
> *The one I love to desert me?*
> *But when I see the score*
> *We still need 34*
> *I can't let selfishness divert me.*

Donald's decision to put side before self is the key to his ultimate triumph. Because he keeps batting, Emma has time to discover the truth about Vincent, and indeed the racing world, as she loses more than just her inheritance to his wiles. The Earl is shocked to the core, but is at least able to take it out on Vincent, in his capacity as Steward of the Jockey Club. St Leger is warned off, banned from all courses for life, a devastating blow. How Donald and Emma are finally reunited, how Vincent is redeemed via his participation in an umbrella-chewer of a last-wicket stand, which wins the match for the Earl, provide an action-packed final ten minutes. If this musical has nothing else going for it, it is short.

If it were ever to reach the West End, *Hearts and Wickets* could be done four times a night, 32 times a week, and 32 different audiences a week would do wonders for the take at the bar. It went down quite well at its world premiere but since 1986 has resided quietly in my files, which may well be the best place for it, even though many of its melodies have since been whistled all over the world. But at least I have co-written a musical about cricket which some impresario may wish to take down from the shelf many years from now, although there could be problems in raising investment for a Broadway production.

I wish I could say that *Hearts and Wickets* had inspired a passion for cricket in my creative team-mate, but regrettably his non-interest has been maintained with steadfast determination. But then I have so many great friends who are cricketing team-mates, it is occasionally refreshing to know that there is a slot in my social calendar where discussion of cricket is off limits. And one of the principal joys of playing cricket with the Heartaches is that very few of them have any interest in musical theatre whatsoever.

www.arundelcastlecricketfoundation.co.uk

Fairfield Books is a specialist publisher of cricket books

www.fairfieldbooks.org.uk